THE TREASURE IN EARTHEN VESSELS

a religion teacher encounters the gospel

by Norm Sharbaugh

Published by

Norm Sharbaugh Ministries
P.O. Box 215
Brownsburg, IN 46112

ISBN # 978-0-9789325-6-5

printed by
Bible & Literature Missionary Foundation
713 Cannon Blvd.
Shelbyville, Tennessee 37160

CONTENTS

ACKNOWLEDGEMENT

I would like to thank my wife, Teri, for her much needed and appreciated work in the typing and retyping of the manuscripts for the book; and also for the many helpful suggestions she has contributed.

I would also like to thank Joy Nespor for suggestions that improved the sentence structure and grammatical part of the book.

DEDICATION

This book is dedicated to my wife, Teri, who has been the source of much encouragement to me; and our 6 wonderful children: Mindi, Julie, Curt, Joy, John, and Evan Robert.

INTRODUCTION

The sky was blue, hedged about by a mass of cumulus clouds. I was five years old sitting on the porch of our house in a part of Pennsylvania that we called Stewart's Hill. This was one of the most exciting days of my childhood. The powers of my imagination were at work. I remember it well. As I looked up into the sky, I began to imagine all types of animal forms in the clouds. I gazed out across the meadow as the wind was sweeping down the hill swaying the wild flowers back and forth. It was one of those peaceful days — a day that caused me to ponder those things around me. I began to ask the questions that philosophers have asked for centuries. I did not word them exactly the way that they have worded them; but in my heart I was asking the questions: Where did I come from? Why am I here? Where did all those flowers and trees come from? Little did I know that it would take me more than twenty years to find the answers to those questions.

We all grow up in some type of religious culture or tradition. In many ways this can be blinding. Some people never question whether their traditions are right or wrong. I think one of the greatest tragedies in the twentieth century is the fact that our traditions have made "religious robots" out of countless millions — people who get very angry when you challenge their tradition because they have never stopped to think out what they believe and why they believe it. The average religious person today has no peripheral vision. He cannot see to the right nor to the left. His mind has been put in a cultural vise. Without questioning he will live with his tradition and die with it.

I was not satisfied with that type of life. I dared to question my religious tradition; and as I did, I noticed that people around me were upset. Yet Jesus on the cross said, *"My God, my God, why hast thou forsaken me?"* The Son of God asked the question "why."

The Bible says, *"Examine yourselves, whether ye be in the faith; prove your own selves. Know ye not your own selves, how that Jesus Christ is in you, except ye be reprobates?"* (II Corinthians 13:5). Do not take a chance on being an eternal reprobate (one who fails the test of being a genuine Christian). Eternity is a long time. It has been estimated that the number of atoms in the human body would equal the number of dried peas four feet thick that would cover 250,000 earths. Suppose also that each dried pea represented a year that we would spend in eternity, if we could talk in terms of time in eternity. At the end of the first year we would throw one pea out in the universe. The second year we would throw out the second pea and so on. There would come a time when the last dried pea on the 250,000th planet would pass through the hour glass of time into eternity. And what would be left? — forever and ever and ever, on and on.

Let me challenge you to follow me with an open mind as I unfold to you how I broke through the tradition barrier into the marvelous light of the glorious gospel of Jesus Christ. This book is my attempt to share how I found peace and how you can, too. I will give my testimony and show what happened when I Biblically questioned my traditions. I will also expose false concepts of the gospel and show the true Gospel and how you can be sure of eternal life. I will close with a challenge to share this Gospel that has been entrusted in earthen vessels.

In this book you will receive the information on how you can determine whether Jesus Christ is in you or whether you are a reprobate.

Chapter One

THE FIRST RAYS OF LIGHT

††

The Bible says, *"But if thine eye be evil, thy whole body shall be full of darkness. If therefore the light that is in thee be darkness, how great is that darkness!"* (Matthew 6:23). If whatever you perceive to be truth is really error, and you think it is light, or truth, then God says, *"Oh, how great is that darkness!"*

We Can Be Deceived

Every man needs to recognize the possibility of being deceived. Everyone of us knows in some way what it is to be deceived. Have you ever bought one of those "midnight specials" on television? It splices, dices, chops, slices and cuts through volcanic rock. You bit and you were sorry.

Life is full of many bitter disappointments in areas where we are deceived. On August 6, 1945, U.S. planes approached the Japanese city of Hiroshima. The people were seemingly unconcerned. Suddenly above the city a parachute was seen.

Thinking that the U.S. planes were in trouble, the people began to cheer. That parachute was carrying the first atomic bomb to be dropped in combat. It floated to 1800 feet above the city and exploded. People at ground zero disintegrated. They were deceived, thinking that there was no danger and found themselves in the midst of the greatest inferno this world has ever known.

Is it possible to be deceived on a spiritual plane? Most certainly! Jesus warned in Matthew 7:22-23, *"Many will say to me in that day, Lord, Lord, have we not prophesied in thy name? And in thy name have cast out devils? And in thy name done many wonderful works? And then will I profess unto them, I never knew you: depart from me, ye that work iniquity."*

Look at what the Apostle Paul said about the nation of Israel. In Romans chapter 10, verses 1-4, Paul said, *"Brethren, my heart's desire and prayer to God for Israel is, that they might be saved. For I bear them record that they have a zeal of God, but not according to knowledge. For they being ignorant of God's righteousness, and going about to establish their own righteousness, have not submitted themselves unto the righteousness of God. For Christ is the end of the law for righteousness to every one that believeth."* Could you picture Paul the Apostle on a modern talk show, stating those convictions?

The host introduces him. "Today as our guest we have the Apostle Paul. Paul, tell us what you believe."

Paul looks into the camera and says, *"As much as I would desire the salvation of my people, the Jew is not saved. He is lost. Sure he has a zeal for God, but he does not have the proper knowledge. He has not submitted himself to God's way of righteousness which is Christ."*

The audience is in an uproar. Groans are heard from one end of the studio to the other. The host takes the microphone and holds it in front of Mr. Average 20th Century Religious Person.

"Paul, how can you condemn anyone who is sincere in their belief. We are all going to get to heaven by different roads; and everyone is entitled to his own opinion." From the sound of the audience you can tell they agree.

If we could just grasp what the Scriptures are actually saying. Your knowledge of salvation must coincide exactly with God's revelation of salvation or you cannot be saved. If we misunderstand the Scripture in this area of salvation there is no hope no matter how sincere we are, even if we are God's chosen people, the Jew.

Paul even went on to say this, *"For I could wish that myself were accursed from Christ for my brethren, my kinsmen according to the flesh"* (Romans 9:3). That word accursed means separated. Paul was really a great Christian, wasn't he?

I cannot say that I feel the same way. But I can say this – that I have a real deep love for my Roman Catholic friends. I was born and raised a devout Roman Catholic, and as such I never questioned anything I was taught. In fact my brother went to a crusade where he heard the gospel preached, and I found out about it. I wound up and knocked him down, boy! Saul of Tarsus Sharbaugh, that's who I was.

The First Time I Questioned My Catholic Faith

I went to St. Joseph's College in Rennselaer, Indiana, run by the Precious Blood Fathers. It was there that I began to question my faith as a Catholic for the first time. One of the events that really caused me to question my faith happened one day in front of the administration building when I was a senior in college. There was a group of priests walking by the administration building. One of them said, "Hey, Norm," and then yelled out one of the sins that I had been confessing in his confession booth. Several of them were laughing. All my life I was taught that they were never allowed to tell anyone what you confessed, and there they were laughing about it.

14

I remember as a boy being taught in one of our catechism classes that a priest had to have the right intention or motive when he administered a sacrament. The Council of Trent, Sess. VII, Can. 11, states "If anyone shall say, that intention, at least of doing what the church does, is not required in ministers while performing and administering the sacraments, let him be anathema." Saint Robert Bellarmine, a Doctor of the Catholic Church, states, "No one can be certain, with the certainty of faith, that he has received a true sacrament, since no sacrament is performed without the intention of the ministers, and no one can see the intention of another." Bellarmine's Works, Vol. 1, p. 488. The implications of this for any sincere Roman Catholic are staggering.

Follow this logic with me. If the priest who baptized the Pope when he was an infant did not have the right intention, then he is not a catholic today. All the priests that he ordains today are not priests and all the sacraments they perform are of none effect for the people. We are on very thin ice if we entrust our souls' eternal destiny in the hands of any mere man no matter what authority he claims. I'm glad that salvation is not in the hands of man for Ephesians 2:8-9 says, *"For by grace are ye saved through faith; and that not of yourselves: it is the gift of God: Not of works, lest any man should boast."*

I thought to myself, "Here I have all my life completely given myself to a system and never once questioned the system." That experience really shook me up.

I Became A High School Religion Teacher

Upon graduating from college, I taught at Catholic Central High School in Grand Rapids. I was hired as a lay religion teacher. But I was reaching a point where I could see that my religion was not practical to me. It had become the source of most of my frustration. My life was not experiencing the love and the joy and the peace that Christ had promised. I did not have the power to experience the Christian life.

I could compare this to a day much later when I was married when our hot water heater went on the blink. My wife, Teri, said, "Norm, there is no hot water."

I replied, "I'll fix it." I began to tear things apart and put new parts on. I put a new switch on it and a new filament, but nothing seemed to work. In the midst of my frustrations my father-in-law walked in.

He analyzed the situation and said, "Did you check the fuse?"

Now I had checked the fuse but because it

looked alright I did not take it out and put a new one in. You guessed it! We put a new fuse in and an hour later we had hot water and a rebuilt hot water heater. The power was there, but it was not getting through. All my life I was taught that the power of the Christian life came through my Roman Catholic Church. However, in experience, I had realized that the church was nothing but a blown out fuse. It was not meeting my spiritual needs, and I was tired of trying to make it work.

Have you ever gone to the supermarket and pulled out one of those carts with the wheels bent in different directions? I have. I pushed it as far as the vegetables and could not take it any longer. I went back and got a cart that worked. Now I could have pushed it through the supermarket and pretended that it was working right. I could have smiled at everyone and kept on struggling.

Tragically, religion works much the same way. You can smile, pretend it works and keep on struggling. Or you can quit trying, knowing it doesn't work, reject all the mechanics of it and still claim the name. You no longer faithfully practice it because you really know it doesn't work, but you go on the rest of your life saying, "I am a Catholic." "I am a Lutheran." "I am a Methodist." "I am a Presbyterian." "I am a Baptist." The family traditions and ties are strong enough for

17

you to retain the name and at least go through all the ceremonies of the baptisms and christenings. I was not satisfied with either of the above.

Liberalism Cracks The Door Open

One summer while I was at Catholic Central teaching, the Christian Brothers, an order in the Catholic Church, were holding a seminar on how to be a better religion teacher. Our school sent us to their workshop. While I was there, for the first time in my life, I heard things that I had never heard before. The church at this time was affected by the liberal philosophies of the day. This liberalism of the philosophy that there is no truth, (as much as I hate that philosophy now), caused a big enough crack in our indoctrination to allow us to get our heads out and begin to think for a change. I heard, for example, my colleagues, fellow teachers, who were priests and nuns, criticizing the pope and saying that he was not infallible. They were tearing down doctrines that I had grown up to believe all my life.

I remember asking one priest there if I could go to confession. We walked around the college campus and as we were walking, he said to me, "Norm, don't become a priest."

I said, "What!"

He repeated, "Don't you ever become a priest."

Then he went on to tell me how unhappy and lonely he was. That week I saw some of the loneliest people I've ever seen in my life. They were confirming my own feelings inside.

I Decided To Find The Truth

When I came back from the seminar, I decided that I was going to find the truth. I said to myself, "They're still looking for the truth. They must not have found it yet, so, I'm going to find it. Surely there is a way out of this maze we call life."

The first thing I did was go to a secular bookstore and buy some philosophy books. I nearly wore out Plato's *Republic*. I read that book till I was blue and the covers fell off. I read one philosopher after another that summer after I came back from the seminar.

A Priest With A Bible

Things really reached a climax when our next teaching semester began. I was in the faculty lounge at Catholic Central High School. In came a Roman Catholic priest who was completely different from many people that I had known. He walked in with a Bible in his hand. He sat down, looked across at me and said, "Norm, do you know what's wrong with us Catholics?"

I asked, "What?"

He replied, "We don't believe the Bible. This book talks about being a believer, and there's a difference in having religion and being a believer."

He was saying that you could be a Catholic and a believer; but just because you are a Catholic, he said, doesn't mean that you are a believer. I thought, "What is he talking about?" I went down to a Bible bookstore and walked in and bought a Bible. I began to study the Bible intensely, and through this study God began to show me some Scriptures that completely contradicted my faith as a Roman Catholic.

Chapter Two

WHAT DID THE BIBLE SAY?

Now let me say this, there were many things in the Bible that supported some of the beliefs that I held as a Catholic. For example, when I read the New Testament I found that Jesus is both man and God. Do you believe that? The Catholic Church believes that and I believe it. The Bible taught the doctrine of the trinity, the virgin birth, the inspiration of Scriptures, and all of those teachings were in agreement with my Catholic faith.

But as I studied the Bible there were some things that were radically different from my Catholic faith. For example, if you were to ask a Bible-believing Christian what his hope is for getting to Heaven, he would say that it is through the work of Christ in His death, burial, and resurrection. Although the Roman Catholic Church claims to believe the same thing, (that salvation is obtained through the death, burial, and resurrection of Christ) the great gulf comes in how you obtain this salvation. The Bible teaches that the work of salvation through the death, burial, and resurrection of Christ is received personally by faith. Each individual must receive Christ personally. Personal faith in Christ echoes through the whole Bible. It doesn't have to come through the "church" or sacraments. As a Roman Catholic I was taught that salvation came through the sacraments.

Good Works, My Church, And The Bible

I was also taught that the work of Christ in His death, burial, and resurrection is not complete, but must be repeated daily; I was allowed to take six of the sacraments to gain the benefits of Christ's work. I could not take the seventh which was holy orders and only a priest could receive that. In order for me to get this salvation I had to get it through the sacramental system. If I worked hard enough and was obedient to all the avenues of grace, I might get to heaven, or at least I would go to purgatory.

But when I read the Bible, I was utterly astounded. The Bible said in Ephesians 2:8 and 9, *"For* by grace are ye saved through faith; and that not of yourselves: It is the gift of God: Not of works, lest any man should boast." I said, "What?" The Bible says, "Not of yourselves." All of my life I was taught that it is of yourself. You have to work hard enough to get it. The Bible says it is not of yourselves; it is a gift. You cannot work for a gift. All you can do is receive a gift. What a blow it was when I realized God would not accept my religion. God would not accept my religiousness, my prayer life, nothing. Listen! If all it took was your prayer life — if all it took was your morality — to get to heaven, Jesus would not have died on that cross. He died on that cross for a reason. It was much more than to establish religion or morality. I will explain this later.

I read on in the Bible and I came to Romans 6:23 which says, "For the wages of sin is death; but the gift of God is eternal life through Jesus Christ our Lord." I read Romans 3:20 that said, "Therefore by the deeds of the law there shall no flesh be justified in his sight: for by the law is the knowledge of sin." Romans 3:28 says, "Therefore we conclude that a man is justified by faith without the deeds of the law." And in Titus the Bible says, "Not by works of righteousness which we have done, but according to his mercy he saved us, by the washing of regeneration, and

23

renewing of the Holy Ghost."

The gift of salvation by faith without works resounded through the entire New Testament as I studied it for nine months as a Roman Catholic religion teacher. I remembered at St. Joseph's College we had a course on the Old Testament Scriptures. But we never had a course on the New Testament. The reason is simple. The Catholic Church is an Old Testament religion with Priesthood and all.

Tradition And The Bible

Another thing that bothered me was that as a Catholic I was taught that tradition was a valid system of truth. But the Bible taught that truth may establish tradition, but tradition **never** establishes truth. Just because a group of people have done something historically for a period of time, does not mean that it is true. A tradition could very well be a false tradition, and that bothered me. For example, I was taught the infallibility of the pope. But when you study the tradition of the hierarchy of the church, you will see that there have been many contradictions. To name just one, Pope Eugenius IV acclaimed Joan of Arc a heretic, and they burned her at the stake. Then in 1919 Pope Benedict XV canonized her a saint. Doesn't that puzzle you? You can go and get some secular history books and you will find the same thing.

On December 18, 1979 the Vatican issued a heresy conviction on theologian Hans Kung because he denied the doctrine of infallibility of church councils and popes. You do not have to be a theologian like Hans Kung to see the contradictions of centuries of popes and councils. In just a superficial study any honest person will come up with the same conclusions. My study in this area started to set me free. The Word of God began to set me free.

I read in Mark, *"Well hath Isaiah prophesied of you hypocrites, as it is written, This people honoureth me with their lips, but their heart is far from me. Howbeit in vain do they worship me, teaching for doctrines the commandments of men. For laying aside the commandment of God, ye hold the tradition of men, as the washing of pots and cups: and many other such like things ye do. And he said unto them, Full well ye reject the commandment of God, that ye may keep your own tradition."* Titus 1:14, Matthew 15:6, and Mark 7:13 taught that tradition caused men to turn from the truth. That bothered my faith right there — because I was told that the Bible should be much thicker. I had been taught that it should be much thicker because of all the councils and papal decrees throughout the history of the church. According to the Roman Catholic Church these decrees have the same authority as the Scripture.

But the Bible is God's complete Book for mankind. It contains all that is necessary for man's salvation. This book does not tell you everything there is to know about God. In fact John the Apostle said that all the world could not even hold all the books if everything that Jesus did was written down (John 21:25). This book tells us about Salvation and how you can personally get to know God.

As I went on, I found that Peter, Paul, and the Lord Jesus always appealed to the Scriptures as their source of authority. II Timothy 3:16 says, *"All scripture is given by inspiration of God, and is profitable for doctrine, for reproof, for correction, for instruction in righteousness."* II Peter 1:19 reads, *"We have also a more sure word of prophecy; whereunto ye do well that ye take heed, as unto a light that shineth in a dark place, until the day dawn, and the day star arise in your hearts."* Acts 17:2 says, *"And Paul, as his manner was, went in unto them, and three sabbath days reasoned with them out of the scriptures."* In Acts 26:22 we find Paul saying, *"Having therefore obtained help of God, I continue unto this day, witnessing both to small and great, saying none other*

Christ Would Not Be A Priest?

Jesus' offering was so complete that in the Bible it says that if He were on earth right now, He would not be a priest. The Bible says in Hebrews 8:4, *"For if he were on earth, he should not be a priest."* Why would He be a priest when there is no longer the need for a sacrifice? A priesthood is necessary only when there is something to sacrifice. Christ was offered once for all forever. It is completed. When He bowed His head, He said, *"It is finished."* It's over; it's done; the battle's been won; the victory's over! He was victorious over sin and death and hell, and all that we can do is receive the gift. That is it! We can add nothing to it; we can take nothing from it. We must accept it.

The Scriptures teach that the sacrifice for our sins was completed 2000 years ago; and because there is no sacrifice today, we do not need a priesthood. In Ephesians chapter 4 and verses 11 through 13 the Bible gives us the ministering offices in their order of leadership in the church. God tells us who are the ministers in the church. The Bible says, *"And he gave some, apostles; and some, prophets; and some, evangelists; and some, pastors and teachers."* But you do not see a priest there. Why don't you see a priest? — Because a believer is the priest. Now every Christian can go boldly unto the real throne of God (Hebrews 4:16).

When you know Christ, you do not need to go to someone else. You can confess your sins to God alone. The Bible teaches us in I John chapter 1 and verse 9, *"If we confess our sins, he is faithful and just to forgive us our sins, and to cleanse us from all unrighteousness."* And by the way, this verse is written to those who are already Christians. Confessing your sins does not save you. Salvation comes through receiving Christ as your Savior. Your salvation is no more or less complete before or after you confess your sins.

Celibacy And The Bible

Next I came to celibacy in the Bible. I saw in I Timothy 3 and verse 2 that the Bible said, *"A bishop then must be blameless, the husband of one wife."* "What?" I said, "How can that be?" It says he is to be the husband of one wife. All my life I was taught that the bishop was forbidden to be married. I questioned, "By what authority have we forbidden bishops to be married all these years when the Bible says that they can be married?" And then I read something that clearly knocked the socks off me. It said in I Timothy 4:1-3 that if anyone forbids marrying or demands abstaining from meats, they are following the doctrines of devils.

Some Startling Discoveries About Mary

I read on and came to some truths about Mary that surprised me. In agreement with the Catholic faith, the Bible teaches that Jesus was born of a virgin. Amen? I believe that with all my heart. But the Bible contradicts the Catholic faith in that Mary was a virgin all her life. The Bible nowhere teaches that. It says that Joseph did not know her till — the Holy Spirit used the word "till" — Jesus was born. And then he knew her, (Matthew 1:25).

In fact, the Bible says in Mark 6:3, *"Is not this the carpenter, the son of Mary, the brother of James, and Joses, and of Judah, and Simon? And are not his sisters here with us? And they were offended at him."* There are a lot of people who have taken this Scripture and said that the word brother there means brethren as they were Christian brethren. But the Greek word that is used for brother is **adelphos** meaning "of the same womb." That's pretty clear, don't you think? It is not talking about brotherhood. It is talking about the physical brother. They came from the same womb of the same mother. Mary was not a virgin all her life. She had children.

Lifelong Teaching About Peter Shattered

As I read on, I found something about Peter that shocked me. All my life I was taught that he was a pope. But Peter himself said in I Peter 5:1, *"The elders which are among you I exhort, who am also an elder."* You see, he did not put himself on a level above anyone else. Did you note that? He said, "I am also an elder." What does the word elder mean? It means "pastor." He was a pastor like any other pastor.

And then in verse three of I Peter 5, the Bible shows that Peter taught that an elder is not to lord it over the flock. That's completely contrary to the hierarchy in the church that I grew up in. The leader is not to lord it over the flock. Then the Bible said in Acts chapter 10 verses 25 and 26, *"And as Peter was coming in, Cornelius met him, and fell down at his feet, and worshipped him. But Peter took him up, saying, Stand up; I myself also am a man."* The Scripture shows that Peter refused homage that was paid to him. But you do not see that today of those who claim to have come from the same line as Peter.

I read in Galatians chapter 2 verses 11 and 14 that Peter was not infallible, for in the Bible Paul said, *"But when Peter was come to Antioch, I withstood him to the face, because he was to be blamed."* And that word "blamed" means that he was wrong — he was wrong in what he was doing. That sure does not look like infallibility.

Changes In the Church — Another Problem

Added to the problem I found in the Bible were the changes in the Catholic Church at this time. I remember as a boy growing up and being taught that we were not allowed to eat meat on Friday. If we did we committed a mortal sin, and if we died in that state we would go to hell. Suddenly we were all granted the option. To eat or not to eat became the question. We were allowed to do something that months and years before would have, under our former religious training, sent us to hell.

There were also the changes in relationship to praying to the saints. The Vatican came out and admitted that many saints who had been prayed to for centuries had never existed. The Latin mass was done away with. The confession booth was underplayed.

As a result of the changes in the church and my study of the Bible, I could not shrug my shoulders and walk away from these contradictions I found in my religious faith. Truth must be systematically consistent. The Bible says that Christ is *"...the same yesterday, and to day, and for ever."* True religion is lining up your mind with the mind of God. The problem was simply this. How could I have confidence in a religious system that proved through all their changes that their mind at one time was not aligned with the mind of God?

When I talk to Catholics today and ask them about certain doctrines in their church, they say, "Well, there are lots of changes in the church today and we do not believe that anymore." My question is, "What proof do you have now that your church has its mind in line with the mind of God?" The frequent reply to this is "Well, all religions have made mistakes and it does not really matter." Tell the pilot of a Boeing 747 that truth does not matter as he is landing his plane and is hit with a down draft. Sure his air speed has been reduced considerably. "Don't worry, Captain, it will all work out at the end." Who is kidding who? That pilot needs to get his plane at an airspeed where he can safely land. Those who didn't care are not here to tell us about it. Their tombstones testify to the fact that truth does matter. To sum it all up, it most certainly does matter what we believe; and in the spiritual realm the unchangeableness of truth is eternal. Why do you think Jesus told the woman at the well that *"God is a Spirit: and they that worship him must worship him in spirit and in truth* (John 4:24)." He didn't say that God was fickle and we could worship Him any way we wanted. Truth is not something you can change through the whims and fancies of some religious leader for the sake of what is expedient for the "church." To keep people in the

34

shackles of religion by putting them on a "spiritual merry-go-round" is the cheapest, dirtiest trick in all the universe. This is undoubtedly the worst form of human exploitation.

Chapter Three

The Road To Calvary

These were some of the problems that I had to candidly face. I did not have the answer yet, but I went on searching. I had each of my one hundred students in my religion classes go out and buy a Bible. It was the blind leading the blind. While we were studying the Bible, one boy in my class came up to me in May and told me about nine steps for salvation that he had in his edition of the Bible. He said, "Mr. Sharbaugh, do you have these in your Bible?"

I said, "No, I don't," and I copied them down, but I did not refer to them right away.

The Cults Move In

Several days later I was walking downtown in Grand Rapids, pondering this search going on in my heart. I saw a sign that said Christian Science. I thought, "Maybe they know what I'm looking for!" So I went in. There was a reading room with two books – the Bible and *Health and Science with Nonsense about the Scriptures.* I remembered the title.

The lady said, "Divine providence brought you here."

I answered, "Yea! Alright! I want to know what I'm searching for."

And they told me that I needed Mary Baker Glover Patterson Eddy's book *Health and Science.* Then they took me to a Health and Science healer (a divine quack-practitioner) up on top of one of the buildings downtown.

When I went in to see him, in so many words I said, "How did you get hung up on this?" He started telling me how he was healed as a boy and I thought, "Maybe there's something to it" and decided to at least give him a chance. I bought her book and read the first page. I said, "Huh?" I read the second page, and I said, "Huh-uh?"

Do you know what? It was the first book I have ever read in my life that made absolutely no sense at all! None! Hey, listen. Anybody that is going to tell me that pain does not exist or that death is not real, that fellow's cuckoo! Can you imagine that? When that fellow knocks on my door, I'm going to get a hammer, and I'll say, "Put your finger out there." Whamm!! And then I am going to say, "Hey! It's not real. Remember? I read it!"

The Devil was really moving in now to keep me from salvation. I was downtown at a bar I used to frequent. I was sitting there with my Bible. I said to the man sitting next to me. "You know, I'm searching, and I don't know what I'm searching for."

He responded, "I know what you're searching for."

I said, "What?"

He replied, "I'm a Mormon. You need the *Book of Mormon*." he repeated.

I thought, "Why all these other books?"

So I went up to his apartment and I will never forget it. We sat down, and he opened the book and told me about his religion. He told me he was going to go out in space someday, become just like God, and create another universe. I said to myself, "Norm, it's time for you to make an exit − stage right − right now." Out the door I went. He did give me the book.

In spite of these books, the Lord used Acts 4:12 to keep me steady. It says, *"Neither is there salvation in any other: for there is none other name under heaven given among men, whereby we must be saved."*

Do you know what was interesting? This Mormon fellow was knocking at my door that next Saturday. Folks, there was not one born again Christian in that town that was knocking on my door trying to win me to Christ – in Grand Rapids, the supposed Christian city. What a tragedy!

The Evangelist
Still searching I went down to a Bible bookstore. I walked in and I said, "Alright, I've been searching for months. What's this store all about?"

The owner took me in his office. I explained that I was a religion teacher up at the Catholic High School. He said, "Wh-wh-wh-wh-what?" And then he said, "What do your priests say?"

I said, "They don't understand what I'm searching for."

But he replied, "Why don't you go ask them?"

Can you imagine a fish jumping in the boat? We talk about being fishers of men, but here's a guy that did not have any hook, line, or anything. I jump right in the boat and he throws me back out. Well, do you know what I did? I went back because I wanted some answers.

This time he said, "Listen, there's an evangelist in the store." So he introduced me to the evangelist who then took me out in the parking lot where we sat and talked in his car. He shared some Scriptures with me.

I said to him, "Sure I'm a sinner, but I'm a good Catholic." He asked me if I had ever received Christ as my personal Savior and I assured him that I had, that I was a Christian, and that he did not need to be concerned about me.

I Faked It

The reality of the whole situation, however, was that I had not really received Christ, and I was not born again. I was not really a Christian. The one word that the evangelist said that got a hold of me was "receive," and God planted that seed in my heart. Yet it was months before that seed came to fruition. I needed the fallow ground of my heart broken up. To do this the Lord used some severe trials brought about by my sins to break my will and bring my heart to the point of surrender.

Religion Does Not Work

There is nothing that can hurt more than sin. I came to the point where I was sick of it. Yet I did not know what to do about it. The one conclusion I came to was that 25 years of religion could not give me power over sin. I could have made excuses for my sin and tried to rationalize it. I could have called it situation ethics into which the morality of our church had disintegrated. But my conscience and the conviction of my heart said it was sin. It was offensive to God and I was powerless to change.

Religion doesn't work. If you really try to live a moral Christian life through some religious system, it is powerless. And of course, much of what I was taught about salvation in the Catholic Church was based on living a moral Christian life. Now I'm all for a moral Christian life, but it is extremely frustrating when there is no power to live it. In fact, some of the most frustrated people I know are people trying to be Christians.

Astronomy Helps

Along with the trials there was another incident that the Lord used at this time to bring me to decision. I taught one science class at Catholic Central. There was a chapter on astronomy, and to prepare for it, I went to the public library and borrowed several books on the subject. One author said that the stars and galaxies seem to have been put in courses predesignated for them. The study of this subject had a real impact upon my life. God took the veil off my mind's eyes and gave me a glimpse of His great eternal power. In the book of Romans chapter one and verse twenty it says, *"For the invisible things of him from the creation of the world are clearly seen, being understood by the things that are made, even his eternal power and Godhead; so that they are without excuse."* I truly got a glimpse of the reality of that verse. I came to see that the universe was not a great colossal accident.

I walked into the museum in Grand Rapids. There on the wall was a mural containing a number of galaxies. A peace settled over me. I thought seriously, and possibly it was the first time in my life that I was really sober about this thought; "There must be a personal God."

Like Cornelius in Acts 10, I was not a Christian and possibly my prayer ascended as a memorial like his did. I knelt down and said, "Father, I know You're real. I know there is a God out there. I don't know how to get to you, but would you get me there?"

I Believed The Gospel But Was Lost

I was invited on July the third to a young lady's house for dinner. She was a Catholic girl I was dating. While at her house, I opened that Bible with the nine steps for salvation that my student in my religion class had given me several months before. As I started to go down that list, I said,

"Yea, I believe that. Sure, I believe that." But you see it's the personal acceptance of Christ that is necessary. All my life I believed that Jesus died on the cross for my sins. I believed that He was buried. I believed that He rose again. I believed it with all my heart. But I was not a Christian — a born again Christian.

You can believe a lot about Christ, but you must make it personal. If I gave you $5,000 and put it in your bank account, you could believe it with all of your heart and then die without withdrawing one penny of it. That is what is happening to salvation today. People say, "Yes I believe it," but they have never come to grips with it personally in their lives; they have never really stepped out by faith and received the great Creator of this universe into their hearts as their Savior.

So that afternoon while at my friend's home, I went over those nine steps. I said yes to the first eight steps and verses that were written down, but the ninth one was puzzling to me. It was Revelation 3:20: *"Behold, I stand at the door, and knock: if any man hear my voice, and open the door, I will come in to him, and will sup with him, and he with me."* I could not get that verse out of my mind. I thought, "What is the door He is talking about?"

Conversion In A Drive-In Movie?

We went to a drive-in that night to see a movie called "The Russians Are Coming." (It was really spiritual.) Sitting there, I began to ponder the Scriptures I had read that afternoon. As I looked out at those stars so perfectly planned that no longer were a colossal accident, all of a sudden the Holy Spirit brought the word "receive" to my mind that the evangelist had given me. I bowed my head. It was 1:25 in the morning on July the 4th, Independence Day. I said, "Jesus, I don't want to sin any more. Come into my heart." That was the greatest moment of my life. I received the Christ that created me. I received Him as my Savior. I, for the first time, did more than just believe **about** Christ. He became **my** Savior.

I began to share the Lord with most everyone. People say, "Norm, I don't know enough to share my faith in Christ." You do not have to be a Bible scholar to share your faith. I was still a member of the Catholic Church and a teacher. A month after I had accepted Christ I went to another workshop on how to teach religion. While I was there, I was sharing how I had accepted the Lord with all the sisters at the lunch table. They looked at me with puzzled expressions.

My Catholic Charismatic Experience

One sister said, "Are you a charismatic?"

I said, "No." Although I had been in the Catholic charismatic movement months before I knew the Lord, I had never received Christ there. The charismatics kept telling me that I needed the baptism of the spirit. They never told me how to be born again — never told me I needed to receive Christ or that he died on the cross for me and that I needed to accept Him as my Savior.

I saw some really bizarre things happen as the Catholic Charismatics met together in Grand Rapids. One lady went on a forty day fast while she was pregnant because she said "the Lord" had told her to do it. Her baby was born with some physical problems. But that did not shake the group at all. They decided that God permitted this so that He could give someone the gift of healing to restore the baby. There is one thing that I have learned in my walk with the Lord. If you divorce horse sense from religion, you do not have much left. Our Lord is a very economical God and He does not play religious games with us.

A Nun Receives Christ

One of the sisters seemed interested so I made it a point to walk with her. I said, "Sister, I accepted Christ! It's real! He's alive! He's seated out there at the right Hand of God! I mean this stuff is real that we've been taught!"

She looked at me like, "Huh?" When I got to the dorm I said, "Listen, I'm going to get my Bible. Have you ever asked Christ to be your Savior?"

She said, "No."

I ran in and got my Bible. I did not know what to tell her. I was still in the incubator. I took my Bible and just opened it. I do not recommend that you do that. You might find yourself chopping your head off or something, with the wrong verse. But I opened it to Galatians; and here is the exact verse I opened it to. I said, "Sister, the Bible says, *'But that no man is justified by the law in the sight of God, it is evident: for, The just shall live by faith.'* (Galatians 3:11)."

"Sister, would you like to receive Christ?" I asked.

She said, "Yes." And folks, her eyes became two puddles, and tears came streaming down her cheeks. She bowed her head on the walk at Niagara University and I saw her receive the Lord Jesus Christ as her Savior. And some of us are afraid to witness because we do not know enough. I did not know anything, but I'll tell you what I found out. If you really want to win people, God will help you. He'll teach you. He'll show you.

So many people get in a rut and think that they will never win a soul to Christ. Just keep at it. Don't quit! For four years I directed Camp Patmos, a youth camp on Kelleys Island in Lake Erie. One summer I heard so much about Lake Erie being the Walleye Capital of the world, I decided to get my license and catch some. I was told how they swim along the shore feeding on minnows in the evening. I fished week after week. I caught bass, catfish, and suckers, but no walleye. By the end of our camp season, I was telling everyone kiddingly that I was writing a book, *The Walleye Conspiracy of Lake Erie*.

The last week of camp Dick, a friend, told me that he would take me out to catch a walleye. The first two hours we were out, Dick caught three and I didn't have a bite. I said, "Dick, how are you holding your mouth." He gave me a silly grin. I tried grinning a while, but that did not work. When it got close to suppertime, Dick asked me if I was going to eat. I said, "No, I'm not going in till I catch something!" Thirty minutes later something hit my line. It was the first walleye I had ever caught. In a little over an hour later, I had caught five.

Leading souls to Christ is much the same way. Just keep at it. If you go fishing every day, you will catch something. It may be a carp or a catfish, but you will catch something. Winning people to the Lord is mostly going. If an incubator baby could lead a nun to Christ, we all can win someone.

What Do I Do With The Catholic Church?

My conversion to Christ now confronted me with some serious decisions. For the first time in my life I was concerned about what God's will was for me. I had to make some decisions concerning my career and the Catholic Church. When Paul the Apostle was converted to Christ on the Damascus Road, he said, *"Lord, what wilt thou have me to do?"* After my conversion, this became the throb of my heart. I became deeply concerned about what God's will was for my life.

In the beginning, I must confess, that my deep emotional attachment to my Catholic friends and the Church itself clouded the voice of the Holy Spirit as He spoke to me. My first desire was to win the Catholic Church to Christ. But I began to see that my presence was saying that I agreed with the church's system of truth even though my spoken testimony was saying that I did not agree with the church's teaching of salvation. My heart became very uneasy about attending mass and going through a ceremony that was crucifying Christ over and over again. I knew what the Bible taught — that Christ's sacrifice for our sins was complete 2000 years ago. There was no need for a twentieth century sacrifice.

I came to the point where I had to make a decision. If it were left up to emotion, I must confess that I would still be in the Catholic Church. All my friends and relatives were there and those ties are very strong. But the Lord brought me to the point in my study of the Bible to realize that principle formed or shaped by truth must be the guiding light of all life. We have lost sight of this in the twentieth century. For the sake of unity, people have become like putty. But it was not so in the beginning. The apostles died because they would not compromise their faith. I'm told if you go to the ancient Roman Coliseums, you will still find the blood stains of the martyrs on the floors and walls of those great arenas. When the Roman government asked those Christians to recant, they said no! In the book of Revelation chapter 2 and verse 13, Jesus brags on Antipas who was His faithful martyr. Antipas would not compromise his faith, and our Lord passed his name down to you and me as a model. He called him *"my faithful martyr."* His blood stains and those of the martyrs through the centuries are a testimony to the fact that their lives were guided by truth, uncompromising truth.

This is not so with people in the mainline Protestant and Catholic denominations today. They have set truth aside for the sake of unity.

The gap between the Catholic Church and my Biblical convictions became so wide spread that I left that church and joined the ranks of those who love and preach the Word of God. To put it simply I didn't change religions; I returned to Biblical Christianity.

In the next chapter I will share some of the mistaken ideas that most people have about the gospel and salvation. I will show some of this "light" that is really darkness.

Chapter Four

COMMONLY ACCEPTED

FALSEHOODS ABOUT THE GOSPEL

We live in an age that is characterized by religious confusion. A television personality, for example, recently said that he wanted to give some of his money to the Lord, but he didn't know how to get it to Him. Today there are television and radio preachers who say they are preaching the "gospel," yet their messages are contradictory.

The Bible, however, gives us a clear definition of the gospel; yet because of the confusion about the truth in this area, before we look at what the gospel is, let us examine some of the false ideas.

Temporal Faith

The gospel is not temporal faith in Christ. Trusting the Lord Jesus to get you from Los Angeles to New York safely is not salvation. I know a lot of folks who ask the Lord Jesus to get them through an operation. They have a temporal faith in Christ. I remember a roommate I had in the hospital. He read pornographic books and told dirty jokes, but prayed to Jesus before his operation.

When I was in the eighth grade we had a basketball tournament in our school. As the field of teams began to narrow down, I prayed harder. One night in particular I knelt down beside my bed and prayed my heart out to the Lord Jesus. We were playing a team that was much bigger than we were. No one in the tournament seemed to like them. I prayed that Jesus would help us beat them, and if He wanted us to win the final game, His will be done. I will never forget that game for the rest of my life. With the score tied and thirty seconds to go we had the ball and were going to work for a last second shot. Jim threw the ball to me. I didn't want it! I threw it back. He didn't want it and gave it back to me. Boy, was I nervous. I gave it back to Jim. He took several dribbles, threw it to me, and said, "Take it!" I threw a shot up, it banked in, and the buzzer went off. We won the game.

If you would have approached me after the game and said, "Norm, do you believe in Jesus?" I would have said, "Of course, I do!" But, in reality, I was not born again. I had a temporal faith in Christ.

You can trust Jesus to get you through the complex circumstances of life and not be born again. You can trust Him to get you through an operation and not be born again. (The Bible says that God's grace falls upon all the just and the unjust. It appears sometimes that the prayers of a nonbeliever are answered when in reality God is extending His mercy — Matthew 5:45.) The gospel is not temporal faith in Jesus Christ. It is more than that.

Let me ask you. Do you have only a temporal faith in Christ? Do you trust Him for everything in this life, but have failed to trust Him for the life beyond?

Love Your Neighbor

The gospel is not love your neighbor as yourself. This is the second and great commandment, but this is not the gospel. To be sure the gospel is a story of the great love of God, but the preaching of love is not the preaching of the gospel.

A religious leader toured our country. He preached to enormous crowds across our nation. The media carried the story that he was preaching the "gospel." I listened to his statements on television, read the newspaper accounts and never once heard the gospel preached. He told nations to cease their hostilities and exercise peace with one another. There was a strong element of "love thy neighbor as thyself" (which is good) in all that he said, but that is not the gospel.

Reformation

The gospel is not reformation. The world views the Bible preacher as a man raining fire and brimstone down on people and telling them that if they don't change their ways they will go to hell. You can change your ways all you want, and you will still go to hell. God is not asking you to reform your life. If that is all we needed, why did Christ die on a cross?

When my wife and I were first married, we were traveling to Grand Rapids, Michigan. I got a flat, pulled over, and changed the tire. The spare I put on needed a legion of angels around it. When we got to the city I told Teri that we would have to buy tires. I searched the yellow pages until I found two recapped "good deals." Two weeks later on the way to Lansing, we heard this enormous thud, thud, thud, thud... It was that "good deal" on the back left. A recap is nothing but putting rubber over an old tire. That is exactly what religion does in the area of reformation. It tries to recap this sinful nature of man. The Bible says that we need a new nature. The gospel tells us how this is accomplished, and reformation is not the way.

The Ten Commandments

The gospel is not obeying the Ten Commandments in order to go to heaven. Scripture says, *"Knowing that a man is not justified by the works of the law, but by the faith of Jesus Christ, even we have believed in Jesus Christ, that we might be justified by the faith of Christ, and not by the works of the law; for by the works of the law shall no flesh be justified."*

What is the real purpose of the Ten Commandments? Romans 3:20 says, *"Therefore, by the deeds of the law there shall no flesh be justified in his sight; for by the law is the knowledge of sin."* The Ten Commandments show us that we are sinners. We can see there is something wrong with us when we fall short of their standard.

My wife has a medical dictionary at home. When our children get sick, she opens the book and attempts to diagnose the case. Sometimes she pinpoints the sickness. The only thing the medical book does is to show us the problem. It does not heal anyone. The commandments give us a knowledge of sin, that we might see our need for a Savior.

It is tragic, but there are scores of people who are trying to keep the Ten Commandments to get to heaven. The Scripture says, *"For whosoever shall keep the whole law, and yet offend in one point, he is guilty of all."* (James 2:10).

I do not know how perfectly you have kept the law. I do know that you are still a sinner. You may not think so, but the Bible says, *"For all have sinned and come short of the glory of God."* (Romans 3:23). That "all" means "all." Somewhere in your life you have sinned and broken one of God's commandments; that sin is enough to cast you into hell. Adam and Eve were cast out of the Garden for committing one sin. The fact that you broke a commandment shows that there is something wrong with your nature which caused you to sin.

When I was a boy we used to take crab apples, put them on sticks, and throw them. One day I bit into one. Boy, was it bitter! (My mouth puckered up for a week.) There were times when a tree would have hundreds of apples on it, and other times when it only produced two or three. But the apples on the tree with only two or three were just as bitter as the hundreds of apples on the other trees. The problem was in the nature of the tree.

A bitter nature will produce bitter fruit. A sinful nature will show itself when an individual breaks God's commandments and sins. You will produce sin fruit; all the commandment keeping in your life is not going to change your nature. That is why Jesus said, *"Ye must be born again."* (John 3:7). You need a new nature that will produce the fruits of righteousness. The Good News is what God did with your sin and how He can give you a new nature.

Let's suppose you obey the traffic laws in your community perfectly for ten years. You never miss a red light, never miss one stop sign, never exceed the speed limit, and always give the proper signals. But on one particular day, you run a stop sign and a police officer pulls you over. What are you going to say when he is writing you out a ticket? "But officer, I stopped at that stop sign for ten years." You are not getting a ticket for that. You are getting a ticket for breaking the law.

How will you plead on Judgement Day where the Scripture says *"the books were opened: and another book was opened, which is the book of life: and the dead were judged out of those things which were written in the books, according to their works."* (Revelation 20:12)?

What are you going to say when God points out some adulterous thought that you have had?

"But, Lord, for ten years I didn't have adulterous thoughts." The Bible teaches that you will have to be eternally punished in hell for that thought.

The point is this. Even if you could live a perfect life from now until you die (very very highly unlikely), you are still going to face God for the sins that you have already committed.

It should be noted at this time that all punishment for sin in the Bible is of eternal duration — *"and the smoke of their torment ascendeth up forever and ever."* (Rev. 14:11). Theodore Parker, though a Universalist, answered thus of hell: "As a Greek scholar and not as a theologian I will say there is no doubt that Jesus Christ taught the endlessness of outer darkness."

There is no way you could perfectly keep the Ten Commandments. That is why you need a Savior. Now you bear with me. In the next chapter I'll show you what the gospel is, and how you can have eternal life.

Good Works

The gospel is not good works. Ephesians 2:8,9 says *"For by grace are ye saved through faith, and that not of yourselves: it is the gift of God: Not of works, lest any man should boast."*

The Good News is not for us to work our way to heaven. If we could do that we would have something to brag about in heaven.

The Scripture says that it is **not of yourselves**. Jesus on the cross said, *"It is finished."* He did all the work and by faith we receive it.

Baptism And Confirmation

The gospel is not baptism and confirmation. If baptism were necessary for salvation, why did Paul say, *"For Christ sent me not to baptize, but to preach the gospel: not with wisdom of words lest the cross of Christ should be made of none effect."*

I was baptized as an infant. Yet there is not one verse in the Bible that shows infant baptism. What does the Bible teach? It shows that once a person has put his faith in Jesus Christ and received Him as Savior, he was then to be baptized. In Acts 2 after Peter had preached the gospel, Acts 2:41 says, *"then they that gladly received his word were baptized."* We see this same pattern throughout the Acts of the Apostles — belief then baptism. Baptism is found in the Bible as a testimony of one's faith in the death, burial, and resurrection of our Lord Jesus Christ. The faith is present before the baptism.

The gospel is not a confirmation ceremony. When I was a boy, we all put our bow ties on and were herded into the Kingdom of God. But the

Bible says that God's Spirit blows where He wills. John chapter 3:7 and 8 says, *"Marvel not that I said unto thee, Ye must be born again. The wind bloweth where it listeth, and thou hearest the sound thereof, but canst not tell whence it cometh, and whither it goeth: so is every one that is born of the Spirit."* This sure is not a liturgical ceremony. Since the event of the cross we do not have to communicate to God in some mechanical way as if we are robots and He is on the other side of the universe.

The "True Church"

The gospel is not the formation of the "true church"; the Good News is not to join a certain church to go to heaven. The Bible nowhere teaches salvation through any church.

What church did the Apostles and the Evangelists in the book of Acts point the people to so that they could be saved? In Acts 8:5 it says this of Philip the Evangelist: *"Then Philip went down to the city of Samaria, and preached Christ unto them."*

He preached what unto them? Christ!

In Acts chapter 2 when Peter preached at Pentecost, what church did he tell them to join? If you study the record you will find none.

What did the men of Cyprus and Cyrene preach

to the people of Antioch? Acts 11:20 says, *"And some of them were men of Cyprus and Cyrene, which, when they were come to Antioch, spake unto the Grecians, preaching the Lord Jesus."* And look what happened. Acts 11:21 says, *"and the hand of the Lord was with them: and a great number believed, and turned unto the Lord."*

What church did Paul tell the Philippian jailer to join to be saved? In Acts 16:28-31 we read, *"But Paul cried with a loud voice, saying, Do thyself no harm: for we are all here. Then he called for a light, and sprang in, and came trembling, and fell down before Paul and Silas, and brought them out, and said, Sirs, what must I do to be saved? And they said, Believe on the Lord Jesus Christ, and thou shalt be saved, and thy house."* In Biblical Christianity people are always pointed to Christ – not a church.

The Word church means "called out ones." When people believed in Christ as their Savior, they were called out of the world. This group of people formed a local church. Today in the Twentieth Century, God is calling people out of the churches of Christendom. In the first three chapters of the Book of Revelation, Christ speaks to the seven churches of Asia Minor. When you study these churches, you will see that they coincide exactly with the past seven ages of church history.

Today we are the Last Church. Here Jesus is on the outside of the church knocking and trying to get the attention of the people on the inside. *"Behold, I stand at the door, and knock: if any man hear my voice, and open the door, I will come in to him, and will sup with him, and he with me."* (Revelation 3:20).

People are in the church worshiping, but they are not worshiping Christ. He's on the outside knocking at the door trying to get the attention of individuals in the church.

I remember the day that Christ got my attention. I was a member of a Roman Catholic Church. I received Christ and was born again. You might be a Methodist, Baptist, Presbyterian, Roman Catholic, or a member of scores of other churches, and Christ has been knocking at the door of your life for years trying to get your attention. He wants you specifically to be born again by personally receiving Him as your Savior – something you have been taking for granted, but in reality, it is something you have never done.

The "Baptism Of The Holy Spirit"

The gospel is not the preaching of the "baptism of the Holy Spirit." I was in the Catholic Charismatic Movement before I was born again. I did not receive Christ as my Savior through any teaching of that movement. I want it understood that I am not a part of that movement. Do not misunderstand me. If anyone is truly saved as a result of reading the Word in that movement, I praise God.

I must emphasize, however, that the salvation that is offerered by Christ as a gift is not a giant "goose bump" – an ecstatic emotional feeling. While I was among the Catholic Charismatics, a man prayed over me, and I had a sensation come over my body like I had never felt before – as if someone took a pan of warm oil and dumped it over my head. At the time I had not received Christ as my Savior, and as I look back, God has assured me in my heart that this particular experience was thoroughly Satanic in origin.

I meet Catholics today who claim a "charismatic experience" that has drawn them closer to the mass and closer to the worship of Mary and the saints. After my conversion to Christ I was drawn farther and farther away from these false doctrines. Obviously we both do not have the same Spirit.

There are hundreds upon thousands of people that think that because they have had some emotional experience, they are saved. The gospel is not an emotional experience through the laying on of hands. The salvation offered through the gospel is not based upon an experience, for how would you

ever know when you had the right experience.
The gospel is based on fact — concrete facts —
whether you feel it or not.

†††

Chapter Five

THE GOSPEL

†††

What is the gospel? A definition of the gospel is found in I Corinthians 15:1-4. Verses 1 and 2 say, *"Moreover, brethren, I declare unto you the gospel which I preached unto you, which also ye have received, and wherein ye stand; by which also ye are saved, if ye keep in memory what I preached unto you, unless ye have believed in vain."* In verse 3 it says, *"For I delivered unto you first of all that which I also received, how that Christ died for our sins according to the scriptures."*

Christ Was Punished In Your Place
The first part of the good news is that Christ took the punishment for our sins on the cross.

You and I deserve to die for our sins, but He died for us. God looked through the portals of time nearly 2,000 years ago and saw every sin that you would ever commit. He put those sins on His Son and punished Him for every one of your sins.

When I was a boy my cousin and I stole peaches from my grandmother's peach tree. Now I had already discovered how physically strong my grandmother was. One day I was helping her weed her garden. She asked me to hand her a cement block that was next to me. I couldn't. She reached out with one hand and lifted it over me to where she wanted it. Well, I had the stupidity to steal peaches from her prize tree. My cousin lived next to my grandma so he got it first. Then he called me up to give me the good news, "Norm, you're going to get it!" I stayed away from Grandma's for months. One day we had a pot luck dinner — at Grandma's. As our family was getting ready to go, I could hear taps playing. When we finally arrived, I hid under the hedges. There was Grandma swinging on the porch swing. I had visions of cement blocks coming down on my head. My cousin came to console me and he said something I have never forgotten. He said, "Norm, Grandma has already given it to me; so I'm going to go up there and ask her to give it to me for you."

Boy, did that sound good. I said, "Go ahead!"

Guess what? Grandma said no! I won't go into the details of what happened to me.

Folks, listen to me. God loves you. Although my grandmother did not accept that proposition, God the Father did accept the work of His Son on your behalf. When Christ came down to earth, God "gave it to Him" for me and you and everyone. *"Christ died for our sins according to the scriptures"* (I Corinthians 15:3). He was punished for every sin that you have ever committed. The death of Jesus Christ alone satisfied God for your sins.

The Bible says, *"And he is the propitiation for our sins"* (I John 2:2). The word propitiation means appeasement. Christ's death was the only thing that would satisfy God for your sins. You could pray a million prayers for penance, and it would not help. There are religious people all over the world praying countless millions of prayers daily to try to appease God. It never has appeased God and it never will. *"And He* (Christ) *is the appeasement for our sins"* (I John 2:2). There are people in the world that go on pilgrimages and literally pray and crawl for miles on their knees from one shrine to another trying to appease God. It has never appeased God and it never will. Your good works will never satisfy God for your sins.

If there was anything that you could have done

to satisfy the wrath of God in punishment for your sins, Christ would not have had to die. In fact, He prayed that very thing in the garden before His death. In Matthew 26:39 He said, *"O my Father, if it be possible, let this cup pass from me: nevertheless, not as I will, but as thou wilt."*

If there had been any other way that your sins could have been taken care of, God the Father would have done it. But there was not. Christ had to tread the winepress of God's wrath for the world. God did not excuse His own Son from the death of the cross in order to show mercy to you and me. His Holy character had to be vindicated and sin punished.

If God did not say yes to His own Son's prayer, do you think that your religious life is going to satisfy His wrath for your sins? Do you think that your prayer life is going to satisfy Him, or your church membership, or your baptismal certificate? Nothing, nothing, nothing will satisfy but the death of Christ.

As a good Roman Catholic, I was taught that Jesus died for my sins, and I believed it; that He was buried, and I believed it; and that He rose again, and I believed it with all my heart. But had I died I would have gone straight to Hell because I was not born again. You might be a good Catholic, or Baptist, or Methodist, or Presbyterian; you believe the gospel — the death, burial, and resurrection of Christ. You believe it beyond the shadow of a doubt, but in reality you are not born again; you are not saved.

Let me explain. Suppose you were drowning and someone threw you a life support — a buoy. It lands in the water in front of you. Let us also suppose that you are a physicist and know about specific gravity. You know that the buoy will hold you up. You believe a lot of good things about it. Are you saved from drowning by what you believe **about** the buoy? No! You had better exercise faith and take the buoy. Faith is trust. Believing about something and trusting in something are two different things.

I remember my first roller coaster ride. It was on one of our school picnics. I had never ridden on a roller coaster and I did not intend to until my friend challenged me. We were in sports together and I did not want him to know that I was "chicken." We got on and I almost choked the poor boy getting the seat belt around us. We went down the first dip. When we got to the top I opened my eyes. Then we went through a tunnel and down a dip that looked like we were going to China.

As we started up the other side Jim nudged me and said, "Norm, guess what?"

I asked weakly, "What?"

"It's the double dip!" he exclaimed.

All my life I thought a double dip was an ice cream cone. Boy, was I in for a surprise. To make a long story short, that roller coaster did pull into the depot.

For years as a young boy I would stand by the railing and watch that roller coaster. Trust in it came the day I got on. Trusting Christ and saying that you trust Christ can be two different things. There has to be a time when you receive Christ and make His work on the cross personal. I have met scores of people who cannot point to a time when they have received Christ. Can you pinpoint a time when you did that?

Burial And Resurrection

One more important thing about the gospel: How do we know that God the Father accepted the death of Christ as atonement for our sins? We know because of the rest of the gospel — the Good News. I Corinthians 15:4 says, *"And that he was buried, and that he rose again the third day."* The resurrection is God the Father's amen to the work of Christ. Acts 2:32 says, *"This Jesus hath God raised up, whereof we all are witnesses,"* and I Corinthians 6:14 says, *"And God hath both raised up the Lord, and will also raise up us by his own power.*" That is Good News.

One night I received Jesus Christ as my Savior by faith in prayer. I said, "Jesus, I don't want to sin anymore. Come into my heart." As a good Catholic, I had believed a lot of good things about Christ. But now it is personal. I made it personal. I received Him as my Savior and now He is my Savior.

Will you do that right now? Be sure that you are saved and born again and heading for heaven. Say this prayer: "Lord Jesus, forgive me for my sin. Thank you for dying on the cross for me. I receive you right now as my Savior and Lord."

Chapter Six

THE TEST OF A TRUE CHRISTIAN

When I was in the first grade at St. Pius Grade School, we had three reading groups: There were the Bluebirds, the Redbirds, and the Blackbirds. I was a Blackbird, the last reading group. The Bluebirds were on page 64; the Redbirds were on page 34; and we, the Blackbirds, were on page 4. I appreciated one friend I had. He was as dumb as I was except he never knew what page we were on. I'd whisper, "Page 4." We almost had it memorized. I think we all stuttered and by the time the year was over, we had run with Dick, Jane, and Spot so much that we were about exhausted.

Nearly every day on the way home I would see Jim, the Rhodes scholar in the third grade who lived down the street. I came home one day and said, "Hey, Jim, look what I learned today. A---- B----."

And Jim butting in said, "Oh that's easy. A B C D E F G H I J K L M N O P."

I thought, "Boy, I'd like to paste him one!"

Now we had a path behind our house that went down over the hill, and there my dad had a coal pile. One day Jim walked down the path over the hill and I thought, "I'm going to fool the Rhodes scholar in the third grade." I ran over and got a shovel and I dug a hole in the middle of my dad's yard. I thought I was going to China. I hollowed that thing out, and then I got some coal off of Dad's pile. I put coal all around the bottom of the hole, around the sides of the hole and I jumped back up on the porch and said, "Oh, here he comes!"

Jim came up the path so I said, "Hey, Jim, when you were gone I hit coal!"

"You hit what? he asked.

I excitedly exclaimed, "I was digging and I hit coal. Come here!" Jim came running. I thought to myself, "See Jim. See Jim run. Run, Jim, run." (Like I said, I was a Blackbird.)

Out of breath, Jim looked down in the hole. Then he went over to the willow tree. I'll never forget it. He broke a limb and cleaned off the leaves. I thought for sure he was going to hit me with it. My mom used to get a stick off the willow tree and I knew what that meant. But he came over there and he said, "I'll show you you're just pretendin'."

"I'm not pretendin'!" I protested.

He yelled, "You are, too!" And he went and scraped the bottom of the hole. Do you know what? He moved all that coal aside and there was just clay. The coal I had stuck on the sides he bumped and it just fell off. He said, "You're pretendin'," and then he went on and gave me a discourse on anthracite and bituminous coal.

I say this reverently. The Holy Spirit comes probing your heart. He came when I was in the Roman Catholic Church; you might be in the Baptist Church, or the Methodist Church, or the Presbyterian Church, or the Lutheran Church. You may not be any religion at all. Maybe you never attend church. And God's Holy Spirit takes the stick of His Word and begins to probe into your heart and He shows you that you're just pretending. You do not have anything of real spiritual value in your heart. You don't have the peace and completeness that accompanies salvation.

Changed Life

Let me quote some Scriptures, and I want you

to pay attention to them. First, if you are a born again believer, you are going to have a changed life. The Bible says, *"Therefore if any man be in Christ, he is a new creature: Old things are passed away; behold, all things are become new."* (II Corinthians 5:17). This idea that you can receive Christ and live like the devil is not found in the Scriptures. Conversion means a new life, Christ's life. The change may not be as dramatic as Paul the Apostle. It may be gradual, but change you will.

Chastised Life

Secondly, you will be chastised by God for sin, if you are a true Christian. If you live in sin, God is going to spank you. The Bible says, *"For whom the Lord loveth he chasteneth, and scourgeth every son whom he receiveth"* (Hebrews 12:6). Don't you love your kids and spank them because you love them? I do. I spank my kids because I love them. Sometimes my kids wish I didn't love them so much.

If you are a born again Christian God **will** spank you for sin. If you slip into a pattern of unconfessed sin, God will get His stick out. I remember a pastor who shared with me about a backslidden Christian who would not get back in fellowship with the Lord. A tornado came through the town and the only house that was demolished was this man's house. I happened to be holding evangelistic meetings shortly after that time. We visited this brother to encourage him to come to our services. I stood in his yard and looked with amazement. I saw one of the biggest trees I've ever seen in my life. It had smashed right through his house. I have heard people say that sometimes God has to hit you with a big stick, but that was the biggest stick I have ever seen in my life. The tragedy of the whole situation was that he still would not get right with God. It sure made a believer out of me. I will be frank with you. If a tornado were coming and I was with that fellow and we were in a building with six foot concrete walls, I would flee him and the building and run to an "outhouse" for safety.

It needs to be said at this point that sin itself can chastize. Some unbelievers are going through hard times because of their present sin. However, it is also true that many go on in sin and get away with it in this life. The Bible says in Ecclesiastes 8:11 *"Because sentence against an evil work is not executed speedily, therefore the heart of the sons of men is fully set in them to do evil."* A non-Christian may get away with sin at least until the judgement, but a Christian never will.

Prayers Will Be Answered

Thirdly, the Bible says if you are a born again believer, you will have your prayers answered. You will not be praying against a stone wall all the time. The Bible says, *"And whatsoever we ask, we receive of him, because we keep his commandments, and do those things that are pleasing in his sight"* (I John 3:22). I must caution on this point. The Bible says in Matthew 5:45, *"That ye may be the children of your Father which is in heaven: for he maketh his sun to rise on the evil and on the good, and sendeth rain on the just and on the unjust."* According to this verse, the grace of God falls on everyone — those that truly are His children and those that are not. I remember a lady that would not accept Christ as her Savior because she told me about the strength of God she experienced at her husband's funeral. I'm sure that God did give her strength, but that is no guarantee that she is a born again Christian, particularly when one cannot pinpoint a time when they accepted Christ as their Savior.

Freedom From The Love Of The World

And then if you are a born again believer, fourthly, you are not going to love the world nor the things of the world and get away with it. The Bible says, *"Love not the world, neither the things* that are in the world. If any man love the world, the love of the Father is not in him" (I John 2:15). This pride-filled world philosophy that elevates man at the expense of God is an abomination. You might say, "Norm, can a Christian love the world?" Yes, but this is what will happen. You will be convicted for it and you will be spanked for it.

Desire To Do God's Will

Next you will have a desire to obey the Lord and to do His Will. When I accepted the Lord, I said, "Lord do you want me to continue to teach here? What do you want me to do?" Before this time the only thing that mattered was what Norm Sharbaugh wanted to do. I wanted to be a great coach. I started in college coaching and I was determined to climb up the coaching rung. When I accepted Christ I said, "Lord, what do you want me to do?" And the Bible says, *"And hereby do we know that we know him"* -- How do we know that we know Him? — *"If we keep His commandments. He that saith, I know him and keepeth not his commandments, is a liar, and the truth is not in him:* (I John 2:3,4).

Now that means if you do not keep His commandments you will be spanked, alright? If you are spanked, that is a sign that you are a Christian.

81

But I'll tell you right now, a Christian will consistently keep God's commandments. You might be bumped around in the beginning of your Christian walk until you learn to get the victory through Christ's power, but you will start down that narrow way of life. You see, the door is narrow. Remember? The way is narrow but it is the only way to experience the abundant life of joy that your heart longs for.

A Love For God

Then if you are a born again believer, you will love God. I tell you, you will love Him. You will not be bitter towards Him. The Bible says, *"We love Him, because He first loved us"* (I John 4:19).

The Witness Of The Holy Spirit

Another test is the fact that you will have the witness of the Holy Spirit inside your breast. The Bible says, *"The Spirit itself beareth witness with our spirit, that we are the children of God"* (Romans 8:16). How do you know that you are a child of God? God's Spirit will bear witness with you that you are. He may do this in two ways: Through the Word of God and the peace of God that will rule in your heart. God's Spirit will point out to you the truth of His Word. If you have received Christ as your Savior, you will also receive spiritual insight to see that the Bible says you are saved and because of the assurance of the Holy Spirit you will believe it. The Bible says *"These things have I written unto you that believe on the name of the Son of God; that ye may know that ye have eternal life..."* (I John 5:13).

I have met a number of people who claim to have received Christ who have no assurance that they have eternal life and are ready for heaven. When the truth of I John 5:11-13 is pointed out they just don't believe it. They say it is too good to be true. It is obvious in talking to these individuals that God's Spirit has not borne witness with their spirit that they are a child of God.

God's Holy Spirit will also give your spirit peace to know that you are His child (the principles of Colossians 3:15). We need to realize at this point that Satan can cause a Christian to doubt his salvation. But it is my personal conviction that at least 60 to 70% of the people that are haunted by the doubts of their salvation are not really born again.

A Love For Other Christians

And lastly you will have a love for other Christians. Preachers will not have to beg you to come to church if you are born again. The Bible says,

"We know that we have passed from death unto life, because we love the brethren. He that loveth not his brother abideth in death." Every once in a while I meet people that hate Christians, but claim to be saved and born again. That is an impossibility.

I remember going door to door sharing the gospel and inviting a community to my evangelistic meetings in a town in Illinois. A lady from a mainline denomination almost tore my head off. Her face was filled with hate toward me, yet she claimed to be born again. I said to her, "Aren't the people from your church friendly?" She almost crawled under the rug. It is tragic that scores of people claim to be born again, but have no love for the brethren.

Did you pass the test? Are you sure that you are a born-again Christian? Remember, everyone will live forever. Be sure that Christ is your Savior. Receive Him right now. Pray "Lord Jesus, forgive me for my sins. I receive you right now as my Savior and my Lord. Thank you for dying for my sins."

Chapter Seven

WANTED –
RANK AND FILE CHRISTIANS
TO SHARE THE GOSPEL

Gibbon, the historian, claimed that the main cause of the rapid spread of Christianity throughout the Roman Empire was the result of an enormous amount of personal work carried on by the rank and file of Christ's followers. This twentieth century desperately needs some rank and file Christians to carry on the Great Commission.

So many of us as Christians are afraid of our reputation, afraid to get involved, afraid of offending our relatives and friends. There is only a handful of Christians today carrying on the work of Christ.

One Wednesday evening my family and I were

85

on our way to church. We had only gone one block when I noticed smoke coming from a neighbor's mobile home. I stopped the car immediately, asked the next door neighbor to call the fire department, and ran to the house on fire. At the top of my lungs I yelled, "Is anyone in there?!" I heard what I thought were footsteps. To the porch I went, hit the door with my shoulder and grabbed the door knob. It was locked.

A neighbor cried out, "They're not home!" I asked, "Does anyone have a hose?" One neighbor did, and I began to spray down the living room where flames began to appear. One man stood back on the walk and criticized me.

By this time a crowd was gathering. I yelled to the people gathering, "Get some buckets of water and some fire extinguishers!" One man brought a fire extinguisher, and we put the flames out in the living room. We then ran to the other window where flames shot out to hit it, but our extinguisher was out of fluid.

If those people standing around would have got some buckets of water and fire extinguishers, the house could have been saved. But the crowd just stood around and watched.

In the church today we have a handful of Christians storming Hell with garden hoses while many of the rank and file stand around criticizing and wallowing in their uselessness.

Get involved. Stick your neck out. Let's face it. You can keep peace in your family by not opening your mouth and witnessing for Christ. But if your relatives do not come to Christ they are going to hell. Remember, Jesus said, *"Think not that I am come to send peace on earth: I came not to send peace, but a sword. For I am come to set a man at variance against his father, and the daughter against her mother, and the daughter-in-law against her mother-in-law. And a man's foes shall be they of his own household. He that loveth father or mother more than me is not worthy of me: and he that loveth son or daughter more than me is not worthy of me. And he that taketh not his cross, and followeth after me, is not worthy of me. He that findeth his life shall lose it: and he that loseth his life for my sake shall find it"* (Matthew 10:34-39).

God is not going to change the nature of conversion for you or anyone. If we become a dedicated useful Christian this world system, which has never been the friend of a Christian, is going to react negatively. Jesus said, *"Remember the word that I said unto you, The servant is not greater than his lord. If they have persecuted me, they will also persecute you..."* (John 15:20).

Francis Hall Edwards in his early days of the

research of x-rays contracted dermatitis caused by x-ray burns. If you work to spread the gospel, there are also some possible dangers to face. You are going to experience the reaction of a self-righteous, sin-filled world against the gospel.

What is needed right now is a generation of committed Christians. The following article once appeared in a London newspaper: "Men wanted for hazardous journey, small wages, bitter cold, long months of complete darkness, constant danger, safe return doubtful, honor and recognition in case of success." This ad was signed by the antartic explorer, Sir Ernest Shackleton. We are told that thousands responded instantly to his call. They were ready to sacrifice their all for a corruptible crown that would one day fade away into oblivion.

The Bible says, *"Know ye not that they which run in a race run all, but one receiveth the prize? So run, that ye may obtain. And every man that striveth for the mastery is temperate in all things. Now they do it to obtain a corruptible crown; but we an incorruptible"* (I Corinthians 9:24, 25).

Commitment means that hesitation is gone. We know what is right; let's do it. There is a need today to stop making excuses because of our fears. Do right. I remember hesitating in a football game in high school. The offensive fullback hit me and smashed me to the ground as the play ran over me. I learned a lesson that day. He who hesitates is lost. It is the same spiritually.

Commitment means that you are not influenced by the crowd. The Scriptures says, *"Thou shalt not follow a multitude to do evil..."* (Exodus 23:2). It is easy to follow the crowd. No one likes to be an oddball. But an oddball you will be in the minds of many if you witness for Christ.

Now I am not saying that we should be tactless and impolite. But many times on our jobs and during the day, God gives us opportunities to give a word of testimony in season and out of season, but the fear of the crowd has given us lockjaw. Remember, the power of the Holy Spirit can unlock that jaw. His power is available to all born again believers.

We in this country do not know what real commitment is for the cause of Christ. I heard an evangelist tell a story of a man who passed a gospel tract out in Moscow and spent ten years in hard labor.

In China years ago communist soldiers came in on an underground church meeting. A picture of Christ was hanging up in the middle of the room. The guards tore down the picture, put it in the middle of the church and said, "You are all going to come and spit on this picture, and deny this

Jesus Christ." The people were instructed that those that spit on the picture were to go to one side of the church. Those that did not were to go to the opposite side to be taken outside and shot.

Several of the elders came first, spit on the picture and denied Christ. A fifteen-year-old Chinese girl was next. She looked up into the guard's eyes, looked at his gun, wiped the spittle off the picture and walked to the side of the church designated for execution. When the communist leader of the soldiers saw the courage of the fifteen-year-old girl and what Christ meant to her, he took everyone out that had denied Christ and shot them dead. He then let the little underground church in that village alone.

You do not have to spit on a picture of Christ to deny Him. Just keep your mouth shut when God wants you to speak. The Bible says, *"For whosoever shall call upon the name of the Lord shall be saved. How then shall they call on him in whom they have not believed? and how shall they believe in him of whom they have not heard? and how shall they hear without a preacher? And how shall they preach, except they be sent? As it is written, How beautiful are the feet of them that preach the gospel of peace, and bring glad tidings of good things!"* (Romans 10:13-15).

No one was ever saved without hearing the

gospel. The gospel must be preached.

Not Everyone Is Going To Heaven

In this business of witnessing and sharing the gospel, you must get personal with people and you cannot take it for granted that people are Christians. Jesus said, *"Enter ye in at the strait gate: for wide is the gate, and broad is the way, that leadeth to destruction, and many there be which go in thereat: Because strait is the gate, and narrow is the way, which leadeth unto life, and few there be that find it"* (Matthew 7:13-14). The masses are not born again Christians, even if they have Christ on the doors of their churches and in their doctrinal statements. We need to sober up to the reality of that fact. All the Methodists are not born again; all the Presbyterians are not born again; all the Baptists are not born again; all the Catholics are not born again. I could go down all the churches of Christendom and say the same thing.

Witness for Christ. The Bible says, *"Quench not the Spirit"* (I Thessalonians 5:19). That has to do with service. In Acts 1:8 Jesus gave His last command: *"But ye shall receive power, after that the Holy Ghost is come upon you: and ye shall be witnesses unto me both in Jerusalem, and in all Judaea, and in Samaria, and unto the uttermost part of the earth.*" If you have accepted Jesus Christ, the Holy Spirit indwells you. The Scripture says, *"Ye are sealed unto the day of redemption"* (Ephesians 4:30). Your body is not redeemed yet. But the Holy Spirit will stay with you through to that day. He indwells you, but the problem is that you are not filled with the Spirit. The evidence that you are filled with the Spirit is not speaking in tongues. It is found in Acts 1:8. *"But ye shall receive power after that the Holy Ghost is come upon you."* And what will be the results? *"And ye shall be witnesses unto me."* If you are filled with God's Spirit you will witness for Christ. You will be sharing the gospel and be concerned about others' souls. You will be involved.

How are you filled with God's Spirit? First ask God to forgive you for not being filled with His Spirit. Then claim the filling as found in Ephesians 5:18. Claim it by faith. *"And be not drunk with wine, wherein is excess; but be filled with the Spirit"* (Ephesians 5:18).

The reason we do not witness for Christ is because we are ashamed of the gospel. Paul wrote Timothy and said, *"Be not thou therefore ashamed of the testimony of our Lord..."* (II Timothy 1:8). That is the problem. We are ashamed to witness for Christ. But thank God for the power of His Spirit. Remember the Word of God says that *"we have this treasure in earthen vessels, that the excellency of the power may be of God, and not of us"* (II Corinthians 4:7).

People have criticized me for giving my testimony as I have by sharing how I came to know Christ as my Savior while I was a religion teacher in a Catholic high school. Yet others, particularly Catholics, need to hear that although I was a faithful Catholic I was not a born again Christian. I'm not saying that all Catholics are on their way to hell. In a religion that boasts of six hundred million I'm sure there are some who are trusting Christ for their salvation. But those trusting their church for salvation are not saved; and for twenty years I was taught to trust my church for salvation. My concern is to shake loose others that follow that same system to a tee and are not born again Christians. Only God knows the hearts of men. But we can't stop witnessing to Catholics, Baptists, Presbyterians, Lutherans, or anyone just because they claim to be Christians.

A distinction has to be made between people who claim a philosophy of Christianity and others that have the Person of Christ. Multitudes claim to be Christians because they have embraced certain teachings of Jesus Christ. Christianity is predominantly a Person not a philosophy or a moral system of truth. To be sure, a true born-again believer will live a moral system of truth based on the Bible but following a Biblical moral system of truth does not make a person a Christian. Receiving the Person of Christ does. I have met scores of people that have embraced a Christian philosophy, but not the Person. They claim to be Christians. They are not.

Speaking of Christ the Bible says, *"But as many as received him, to them gave he power to become the sons of God, even to them that believe on his name"* (John 1:12). It is not receiving principles about Christ, but the Person of Christ that brings salvation. Theology never saved a soul. I'm sure there are people in hell right now who know their catechisms from cover to cover. They may know all the right theology, but they have never received the Person of Christ.

Look at Paul the Apostle's conversion on the road to Damascus. He did not surrender to a philosophy that day but a Person. Jesus became his Lord that day (Acts 9:6).

Let me warn you now. If by God's grace you determine to be a witness for Christ, you are going to enter the arena of criticism. You are going to have to stick your nose in other people's religious business. Pay the price. Do it. It will be worth it all. God says in Daniel, *"And they that be wise shall shine as the brightness of the firmament; and they that turn many to righteousness as the stars for ever and ever"* (Daniel 12:3).

We have all seen stars come and go. The baseball stars of the fifties are not the stars of the sixties and seventies. The football and basketball stars of yesterday are not the stars of today. But God says that those that turn many to righteousness shall shine as stars forever.

ΨΨΨΨΨΨΨΨΨΨΨΨΨΨΨΨΨΨΨΨΨΨΨΨΨΨΨΨΨ

Chapter Eight

A PERSONAL APPEAL

ΨΨΨΨΨΨΨΨΨΨΨΨΨΨΨΨΨΨΨΨΨΨΨΨΨΨΨΨΨ

I believe the truth of what I have tried to express in this book is so eternally important that I have chosen to close with one last appeal for you to receive Christ as your Savior. Let's look at this subject one last time.

If there was a way for you to have all of your sins past, present, and future, eternally forgiven, would you take that way? The Bible teaches that you can make a decision today and place yourself eternally in the hand of God. You can be in a "state of grace" from this day forward and forever.

What Does The Bible Teach?

The Bible teaches that God is Holy and must punish sin. *"The wages of sin is death"* (Romans 6:23). The word death here conveys the idea of spiritual and eternal separation from God – punishment in the lake of fire for eternity. *"And the smoke of their torment ascendeth up for ever and ever"* (Revelation 14:11).

But Why?

You might ask, "Why does God have to punish us?" God is unchangeable and holy. *"I am the Lord, I change not"* (Malachi 3:6). *"Holy, holy, holy, is the Lord of host"* (Isaiah 6:3). God's holy and unchangeable character demands that sin and rebellion be punished. There is no human way out. Your sins must be eternally punished. God just can't wink at our sin and forget it.

One summer while I was traveling, a state trooper pulled me over. He told me I was speeding, asked for my driver's license and registration, and began to walk back to his police cruiser. In desperation I leaned out of the car and asked if he would just give me a warning. He asked how my record was and I told him that it was very good.

A few minutes later he walked back and said, "I'm going to give you a warning. I noticed that you slowed down before you ever knew that I was there." (When I saw how fast I was going I did take my foot off the accelerator, but I still broke the law.) He continued, "We don't give many warnings in this state."

Very graciously I thanked him and drove off rejoicing. Now before I turn this into an illustration I want to say something. (If you are a police officer and you're reading this I want you to know something: I love you man!) I was very grateful that I did not have to pay the $85.00 fine. It was completely acceptably within his power to extend human mercy to me. We all accept that concept, especially if we are on the receiving end of it.

98

God Also Extends Mercy

Now God also extends mercy, but there is a difference. God is bound by his holy character.

In the above illustration, if the law was going to be upheld someone would have to pay that fine. Many of man's laws are not upheld. Many judges are responsible for abusing our laws. A correctional officer in Florida told me of a teenager that was finally put in jail after his 32nd offence. He had broken the law 31 times and was released. God is not that way. The $85.00 fine, so to speak, must be paid. If you and I pay for our sins we must go to hell and Gehenna forever.

God, however, in his abundant mercy and grace found a way for the whole human race to be saved from the eternal consequences of our sins. He sent His Son to take the full punishment for your sins. All of your sins – past, present, and future – were placed on Jesus Christ 2,000 years ago. He paid your sin debt in full. The Scripture says that He bore *"our sins in his own body on the tree..."* God's holy law was vindicated and upheld because Christ paid the sin debt, that we all owe.

Another Look At This Subject

Let's back up a moment and take another run at this. Now, I'm not trying to be silly, but if you were to ask me "Why does water have two parts hydrogen to one part oxygen," I would have to answer, "Because water has two parts hydrogen to one part oxygen." In other words, that is its nature.

God's Holy nature demands that sin be punished. That is an unchangeable fact -- a fact that makes Hell a reality. You might respond by saying, "That's not fair." It appears that way from a human viewpoint. We "all have sinned, and come short of the glory of God," (Romans 3:23) and even if we could never sin again from this moment on, we would still go to Hell for our past sins. But God is not sending the human race down a one way street of doom and disaster. He, in His eternal love, offers us an alternative.

The Alternative

The Bible teaches that *"the gift of God is eternal life through Jesus Christ our Lord"* (Romans 6:23).

God can offer you eternal life and in no way contradict His Holy, unchangeable character because of what His Son, Jesus Christ, did for you nearly 2,000 years ago.

What Did Christ Do?

"Christ died for our sins according to the scriptures" (I Corinthians 15:3). What in the world does that mean? How do you view Christ's death? A preacher, Evangelist T. T. Martin, once gave this illustration. Let's imagine you were sitting on a pier in Florida fishing. Suddenly a man runs down the pier, shouts, "I love you," jumps into the water and drowns. The entire episode would certainly be weird and unrelated.

That is precisely how the average person views the death of Christ on the cross. When someone says, "Christ died for you," the average person has been programmed to get religious, look very sanctimonious, nod their head in agreement, and not have the foggiest idea of what that truly means.

Now let's suppose you are fishing and you fall into the water. Just as you are about to drown, a man leaps into your peril, grabs you, takes you to shore and saves your life. You would know that this man cares about you. The Bible teaches that Christ died for your sins according to the Scriptures.

Christ put himself in your predicament, and as He looked through the portals of time, He saw YOU and took the punishment for every one of YOUR sins. He allowed His Father, who is unchangeable and must punish sin, to punish Him for your sins.

As a boy growing up in the Roman Catholic faith, my religious leaders told me countless times that Jesus died for my sins on the cross, that He was punished for my sins and then they would turn around and in essence teach that I had to atone for my own sins by penances, prayers, good works, sacraments, fastings, novenas, and doing all sorts of other religious things that made me totally dependent on the church for salvation and not on Christ.

The Choice

Let's imagine now that the same police officer that pulled me over pulls you over and gives you an $85.00 fine, and I ask if I could accompany you when you go to pay it. As you stand before the clerk to pay your fine, broke and without a dime in your pocket, I step up and offer to pay it for you. You now have a choice. You can either let me pay the fine, or you will have to pay it.

God Will Not Force Salvation On Anyone

God gives you the same choice with the punishment that He requires for your sins. You can either accept His payment, when His Son was punished for all of your sins; or you can be like the majority of the human race and because of pride and unbelief, refuse God's gift and take

101

your own punishment for your sins. *"The wages of sin is death, but the gift of God is eternal life through Jesus Christ our Lord"* (Romans 6:23). Are you taking a chance on eternity? The Bible says, *"But as many as received him, to them gave he power to become the sons of God, even to them that believe on his name"* (John 1:12). The Word of God clearly teaches that you can have eternal life now. In I John 5:11-13 the Scripture says, *"And this is the record, that God hath given to us eternal life, and this life is in his Son. He that hath the Son hath life; and he that hath not the Son of God hath not life. These things have I written unto you that believe on the name of the Son of God; that ye may know that ye have eternal life, and that ye may believe on the name of the Son of God."*

Did you note what it said? *"...That ye may know that ye have eternal life."* You do not wait until you die to find out.

Salvation Is Of Christ And Christ Alone

Jesus said in John 14:6, *"I am the way, the truth, and the life: no man cometh unto the Father, but by me."*

Tragically, man-made religions come along and say, "It's not just Jesus, it's Jesus and sacraments; Jesus and my church, Jesus and Mary; Jesus and good works; Jesus and thousands of prayers."

No! What does the Scripture say? *"To as many as received Him;" "I am the way, the truth, and the life;" "He that hath the Son hath life."* (John 1:12; John 14:6; I John 5:12)

Look at what the Bible says in Acts 8:5, *"Then Philip went down to the city of Samaria and preached Christ unto them."* In the same chapter look at what Philip the

Evangelist preached to the Ethiopian eunuch: *"Then Philip opened his mouth and began at the same scripture, and preached unto him Jesus."*

The point I'm making through all of this is that salvation is faith in Christ alone. What you have to do right now is transfer your faith from sacraments, the church, Mary, good works, prayers and penances and place your faith in Christ alone as your salvation.

Christ Appeased God's Wrath

Consider these two Scriptures with me. The Bible says in I John 2:2, *"And he is the <u>propitiation</u> for our sins: and not for ours only, but also for the sins of the whole world."*

Look also at I John 4:10. *"Herein is love, not that we loved God, but that he loved us, and sent his son to be the <u>propitiation</u> for our sins."* (Romans 3:25 also)

What does the word propitiation mean? It means to appease and satisfy God's wrath for our sins. The Scripture records that Christ's death on the cross was the only thing that satisfied the wrath of God for our sins. Our prayers, good works, and other religious deeds did not and will not satisfy God's wrath for our sin. The simple truth is that Christ is our salvation. After you become a Christian by faith in Christ alone there are some things that Christ asks us to do, but these do not add to your salvation.

Be Sure Of Eternity – Receive Christ

God loves you and has already done the work to get you to heaven. It is not work you do. It is work that He has done. Jesus bowed his head and said. *"It is finished."* Will you be a partaker of this finished work of Christ?

If you are concerned about the destiny of your soul and

would like to accept Christ's payment for your sins and the gift of eternal life, ask God to forgive you for your sins and receive Jesus Christ as your Savior. You could pray the following:

"Lord Jesus, I ask that you forgive me for my sins and I receive you alone as my Savior and my Lord. Thank you for dying on the cross for me. I choose to transfer all of my faith from my religious efforts and works to You and Your finished work on the cross alone as my soul's salvation."

Dear Reader,
    Following this chapter is a Bible study composed of many of the questions that I had as I first intensely searched the Scripture. The Biblical answers from these questions set me free to receive Christ as my Savior.
    I would like to encourage you to continue through this Bible study.

VITAL STUDIES
IN THE
SCRIPTURES

VITAL STUDIES
IN THE SCRIPTURES

Part 1
WHAT IS OUR AUTHORITY?

1. How is all Scripture given? *(II Timothy 3:16 "All scripture is given by inspiration of God, and is profitable for doctrine, for reproof, for correction, for instruction in righteousness.")*

2. How is Scripture profitable and useful? *(II Timothy 3:16 above)*

3. To what can the Scripture lead us? *(II Timothy 3:15 "And that from a child thou hast known the holy scriptures, which are able to make thee wise unto salvation through faith which is in Christ Jesus.")*

4. What does Scripture do for the man of God? *(II Timothy 3:17 "That the man of God may be perfect, thoroughly furnished unto all good works.")*

5. A man of God who knows the Scriptures can be equipped for how many good works? *(II Timothy 3:17 above)*

6. What do you think that indicates about the Scriptures?

7. To what does Peter tell us to pay attention? *(II Peter 1:19 "We have also a more sure word of prophecy; whereunto ye do well that ye take heed, as unto a light that shineth in a dark place, until the day dawn, and the day star arise in your hearts.")* (note: The word "prophecy" refers to the Scriptures.)

8. How were the holy men of God moved when they gave us prophecy or the Scripture? *(II Peter 1:21 "For the prophecy came not in old time by the will of man: but holy men of God spake as they were moved by the Holy Ghost.)*

9. What did Paul appeal to as the source of his authority? *(Romans 4:3 "For what saith the scripture? 'Abraham believed God, and it was counted unto him for righteousness.'")*

10. What did Jesus appeal to as a source of authority when He taught men? *(Luke 24:27 "And beginning at Moses and all the prophets, he expounded unto them in all the scriptures the things concerning himself.")*

11. What did Jesus appeal to in His conquest over Satan? *(Matthew 4:4-7 "But he answered and said, It is written, Man shall not live by bread alone, but by every word that proceedeth out of the mouth of God. Then the devil taketh him up into the holy city, and setteth him on a pinnacle of the temple, and saith unto him, If thou be the Son of God, cast thyself down:*

for it is written, He shall give his angels charge concerning thee: and in their hands they shall bear thee up, lest at any time thou dash thy foot against a stone. Jesus said unto him, It is written again, Thou shalt not tempt the Lord thy God.") (For more Scripture refer to verses 8-10)

12. Why did Jesus rebuke the Sadducees? *(Matthew 22:29 "Jesus answered and said unto them, Ye do err, not knowing the scriptures, nor the power of God.")*

13. What did the tradition of the Scribes and Pharisees cause them to do to the commandments of God? *(Mark 7:8 "For laying aside the commandment of God, ye hold the tradition of men...")*

14. What kind of worship will the doctrines or dogmas of men produce? *(Mark 7:7 "Howbeit in vain do they worship me, teaching for doctrines the commandments of men.")* (also refer to Matthew 15:9)

15. What did traditions do to the commandment and Word of God? *(Matthew 15:6b "...Thus have ye made the commandment of God of none effect by your traditions.")* (also refer to Mark 7:13)

16. The commandments of men cause us to turn from what? *(Titus 1:14 "Not giving heed to Jewish fables, and commandments of men, that turn from the truth.")*

17. What can philosophy and tradition do to us?
(Colossians 2:8 "Beware lest any man spoil you through philosophy and vain deceit, after the tradition of men, after the rudiments of the world, and not after Christ.")

Part 2

WHAT IS THIS SACRIFICE ALL ABOUT?

1. Could the sacrifice of bulls and goats in the Old Testament take away sins? *(Hebrews 10:11 "And every priest standeth daily ministering and offering oftentimes the same sacrifices, which can never take away sins.")* (also refer to Hebrews 10:4)

2. What did these sacrifices bring to remembrance every year? *(Hebrews 10:3 "But in those sacrifices there is a remembrance again made of sins every year.")*

3. Who is the real lamb of God? *(John 1:29 "The next day John seeth Jesus coming unto him, and saith, Behold the Lamb of God, which taketh away the sin of the world.")*

4. What was the purpose of the real lamb of God? *(John 1:29 above)*

5. What has to be shed for sins to be forgiven? *(Hebrews 9:22 "And almost all things are by the law purged with blood; and without shedding of blood is no remission.")*

6. How many times does Christ have to be offered up for our sins? *(Hebrews 7:27 "Who needeth not daily, as those high priests, to offer up sacrifice, first for his own sins, and then for the people's: for this he did once, when he offered up himself.")* (also refer to Hebrews 10:10, 12)

7. How long does the value of the sacrifice of Christ's death for our sins last? *(Hebrews 10:14 "For by one offering he hath perfected for ever them that are sanctified.")*

8. How long does the value of the redemption that Christ gained for us by his one sacrifice last? *(Hebrews 9:12 "Neither by the blood of goats and calves, but by his own blood he entered in once into the holy place, having obtained eternal redemption for us.")*

9. How are we justified (pronounced righteous)? *(Romans 5:9 "Much more then, being now justified by his blood, we shall be saved from wrath though him.")*

10. The blood of Christ cleanses us from how much sin? *(I John 1:7 "But if we walk in light, as he is in the light, we have fellowship with one another, and the blood of Jesus Christ his Son cleanseth us from all sin.")*

11. Considering the above Scriptures and your answers, is there a need for any other sacrifice for sins other than what Christ performed at Calvary?

110

12. If there is no need for another sacrifice, is there any need for a New Testament priesthood?

13. If Christ were on earth would He be a priest? *(Hebrews 8:4 "For if he were on earth, he should not be a priest, seeing that there are priests that offer gifts according to the law.")*

14. Ephesians 4:11-12 gives us the ministering offices in the church. Does it say anything about a priest? *(Ephesians 4:11-12 "And he gave some, apostles; and some, prophets; and some, evangelists; and some, pastors and teachers; for the perfecting of the saints, for the work of the ministry, for the edifying of the body of Christ.")*

15. Who is the Christian's priest? *(Hebrews 4:14 "Seeing then that we have a great high priest, that is passed into the heavens, Jesus the Son of God, let us hold fast our profession.")*

16. Who is the only one sufficient to go to God for us? *(I Timothy 2:5 "For there is one God, and one mediator between God and men, the man Christ Jesus.")*

17. Where is this priest at this moment? *(Hebrews 8:1 "Now of the things which we have spoken this is the sum: We have such an high priest, who is set on the right hand of the throne of the Majesty in the heavens.")* (also refer to Hebrews 4:14)

18. What does He do in heaven for us? *(I John 2:1*

"My little children, these things write I unto you, that ye sin not. And if any man sin, we have an advocate with the Father, Jesus Christ the righteous.")

19. Should you call anyone Father in a spiritual sense on earth? *(Matthew 23:9 "And call no man your father upon the earth: for one is your Father, which is in heaven.")*

20. Jesus priesthood was far superior than the priesthood of men. Name three reasons why this is true. *(Hebrews 7:23, 24, 27 "And they truly were many priests, because they were not suffered to continue by reason of death: But this man, because he continueth ever, hath an unchangeable priesthood....Who needeth not daily, as those high priests, to offer up sacrifice, first for his own sins, and then for the people's: for this he did once, when he offered up himself.") Hebrews 10:11, 12 "And every priest standeth daily ministering and offering oftentimes the same sacrifices, which can never take away sins. But this man, after he had offered one sacrifice for sins for ever, sat down on the right hand of God.")*

21. Can a bishop be married? *(I Timothy 3:2 "A bishop then must be blameless, the husband of one wife, vigilant, sober, of good behavior, given to hospitality, apt to teach.")*

22. What right did Paul claim if he so chose? *(I Corinthians 9:5 "Have we not power to lead about a sister, a wife, as well as other apostles, and as the brethren of the Lord and Cephas?")*

23. What does Matthew 8:14 indicate about Peter? *(Matthew 8:14 "And when Jesus was come into*

112

Peter's house, he saw his wife's mother laid, and sick of a fever.")

24. **In I Timothy 4:1-3 what is the source behind the doctrine that forbids marriage?** *(I Timothy 4:1-3 "Now the Spirit speaketh expressly, that in the latter times some shall depart from the faith, giving heed to seducing spirits, and doctrines of devils; speaking lies in hypocrisy; having their conscience seared with a hot iron; forbidding to marry, and commanding to abstain from meats, which God hath created to be received with thanksgiving of them which believe and know the truth.")*

25. **Does the Bible ever speak in a figurative sense?** (refer to John 10:9; 15:1; Revelation 1:20; Matthew 13:38; I Corinthians 10:4; Genesis 41:26; Daniel 7:24)

    Did Jesus become a door or gate in John 10:9? *(John 10:9 "I am the door: by me if any man enter in, he shall be saved, and shall go in and out, and find pasture.")*

    Did Jesus become a vine in John 15:1? *(John 15:1 "I am the true vine and my Father is the husbandman.")*

    Were the seven stars in Revelation 1:20 literally stars or did they represent angels? *(Revelation 1:20 "The mystery of the seven stars which thou sawest in my right hand, and the seven golden candlesticks. The seven stars are the angels of the seven churches: and the seven candlesticks which thou sawest are the seven churches.")*

26. **Of what is the Lord's Supper a memorial?** *(I Corinthians 11:26 "For as often as ye eat this bread, and drink this cup, ye do show the Lord's death till he come.")*

27. **Why are we to partake of the Lord's Supper?** (See I Corinthians 11:26 above)

Part 3

PETER, PAUL, AND MARY

1. ### What office did Peter hold in the church?
   (I Peter 5:1 *"The elders which are among you I exhort, who am also an elder, and a witness of the sufferings of Christ, and also a partaker of the glory that shall be revealed."* (Elder - one who had the spiritual care of a local church. There were a number of elders in each church.)

2. ### Does the Bible teach that anyone of the apostles was to receive homage and be exalted above the others? *(Matthew 23:11 "But he that is greatest among you shall be your servant.")*

3. ### What did Jesus teach should be our attitude in ministering to others? (Matthew 20:26 *"But it shall not be so among you: but whosoever will be great among you, let him be your minister.")*

4. ### Did Peter want homage paid to him? *(Acts 10:25-26 "And as Peter was coming in, Cornelius met him, and fell down at his feet, and worshipped him. But Peter took him up, saying, Stand up; I myself also am a man.")*

5. ### What was Peter's attitude toward the people he ministered to? *(I Peter 5:3 "Neither as being lords over God's heritage, but being ensamples to the flock.")*

6. In I Peter 5:1 does Peter claim a higher position than the other elders? *(I Peter 5:1 previous page)*

7. What is his relationship with the other elders? *(I Peter 5:1 previous page)*

8. Did Peter claim anything extraordinary about his person? *(Acts 10:25-26 previous page)*

9. Does God play favorites? *(Galatians 2:6 "But of these who seemed to be somewhat, (whatsoever they were, it maketh no matter to me: God accepteth no man's person:) for they who seem to be somewhat in conference added nothing to me.")*

10. Did Peter teach that God shows partiality? *(Acts 10:34 "Then Peter opened his mouth, and said, Of a truth I perceive that God is no respecter of persons.")*

11. Did Peter work among the Jews or the Gentiles? *(Galatians 2:8 "For he that wrought effectually in Peter to the apostleship of the circumcision, the same was mighty in me toward the Gentiles.")* (Circumcision refers to Jews.)

12. At what city does Peter write his epistle from? *(I Peter 5:13 "The church that is at Babylon, elected together with you, saluteth you; and so doth Marcus my son.")*

115

13. When Paul wrote his letter to Rome did he
    address it to anyone in particular in authority
    ministering there? *(Romans 1:7 "To all that be in Rome,
    beloved of God, called to be saints: Grace to you and peace from
    God our Father, and the Lord Jesus Christ.")*

14. In the 16th chapter of Romans, Paul sent
    greetings to 27 people by name including
    some women, and several groups. Does he
    mention Peter at all? *(Romans 16:1-27)*

15. What is another name for Peter? *(John 1:42
    "And he brought him to Jesus. And when Jesus beheld him, he
    said, Thou art Simon the son of Jona: thou shalt be called
    Cephas, which is by interpretation, A stone.")*

16. Was Peter infallible? *(Galatians 2:11, 14 "But when
    Peter was come to Antioch, I withstood him to the face, because
    he was to be blamed...But when I saw that they walked not
    uprightly according to the truth of the gospel, I said unto Peter
    before them all, If thou, being a Jew, livest after the manner of
    Gentiles, and not as do the Jews, why compellest thou the
    Gentiles to live as do the Jews?"*

17. Did Mary need a Savior? *(Luke 1:46-47 "And Mary
    said, My soul doth magnify the Lord, and my spirit hath rejoiced
    in God my Saviour.")*

18. What does the Bible teach about all men?
    (Romans 3:10, 23 "As it is written, There is none righteous, no,

not one...For all have sinned, and come short of the glory of God.")

19. Who did Mary tell men to listen to" *(John 2:5*
"His mother saith unto the servants, Whatsoever he saith unto you, do it.")

20. According to the Scriptures can there be any other mediator between God and man other than Jesus Christ? *(I Timothy 2:5 "For there is one God, and one mediator between God and men, the man Christ Jesus.")*

21. Who is the only person that can take us to the Father? *(John 14:6 "Jesus saith unto him, I am the way, the truth, and the life: no man cometh unto the Father, but by me.")*

22. Who is our advocate or lawyer in Heaven? *(I John 2:1 "My little children, these things write I unto you, that ye sin not. And if any man sin, we have an advocate with the Father, Jesus Christ the righteous.")*

23. Who makes intercession for us? *(Romans 8:34 "Who is he that condemneth? It is Christ that died, yea rather, that is risen again, who is even at the right hand of God, who also maketh intercession for us.")*

24. What is the only name whereby we can be saved? *(Acts 4:11-12 "This is the stone which was set at nought of you builders, which is become the head of the corner. Neither is there salvation in any other: for there is none other*

name under heaven given among men, whereby we must be saved.")

25. How was Jesus conceived within Mary? *(Matthew 1:20 "But while he thought on these things, behold, the angel of the Lord appeared unto him in a dream, saying, Joseph, thou son of David, fear not to take unto thee Mary thy wife: for that which is conceived in her is of the Holy Ghost."*

26. What was Mary even up to the point of the conception of Christ? *(Matthew 1:23 "Behold, a virgin shall be with child, and shall bring forth a son, and they shall call his name Emmanuel, which being interpreted is, God with us.")*

27. After the birth of Christ what do you think the word "till" or "before" indicates in Matthew 1:25? *(Matthew 1:24, 25 "Then Joseph being raised from sleep did as the angel of the Lord had bidden him, and took unto him his wife: And knew her not till she had brought forth her firstborn son: and he called his name Jesus.")*

28. Does Matthew 1:24-25 indicate that Joseph had no relations with his wife after Jesus was born? *(Matthew 1:24-25 above)*

29. Did Jesus have other brothers and sisters? *(Mark 6:3 "Is not this the carpenter, the son of Mary, the brother of James, and Joses, and of Judah, and Simon? And are not his sisters here with us? An they were offended at him." Galatians 1:19 "But other of the apostles saw I none, save James the Lord's brother." Matthew 12:46, 47 "While he yet talked to the people, behold, his mother and his brethren stood*

118

without, desiring to speak with him. Then one said unto him, Behold,
thy mother and thy brethren stand without, desiring to speak with
thee.")

30. Did Jesus brothers or brethren believe in Him
    while He was in His public ministry? *(John 7:5*
    "For neither did his brethren believe in him.") (The work brethren
    has been passed off by some to mean simply other Christians as in a
    Christian sense we are His brethren. But how could these people be
    brethren in a Christian sense when they did not believe in Him? There is
    no way they could be brothers in a spiritual sense unless they believed.
    Could it be that the Scriptures are emphasizing that not even those in
    Jesus immediate family believed in Him?)

Part 4

WHERE DOES THE CHURCH APPEAR?

1. Read chapter 2 of Acts in which the first
   Christian church was founded. Was Rome the
   first church? *(Acts 2:5, 14, 41 "And there were dwelling at*
   Jerusalem Jews, devout men, out of every nation under heaven...
   But Peter, standing up with the eleven, lifted up his voice, and
   said unto them, Ye men of Juda ea, and all ye that dwell at
   Jerusalem, be this known unto you, and hearken to my
   words...Then they that gladly received his word were baptized:
   and the same day there were added unto them about three
   thousand souls.")

2. What city saw the formation of the first
   church? *(Acts 2:5, 14 above)*

3. Where were some other local churches founded? *(I Corinthians 1:2a "Unto the church of God which is at Corinth." Galatians 1:2 "And all the brethren which are with me, unto the churches of Galatia." I Thessalonians 1:1 "Paul, and Silvanus, and Timothy, unto the church of the Thessalonians which is in God the Father and in the Lord Jesus Christ: Grace be unto you, and peace, from God our Father, and the Lord Jesus Christ."*

Part 5

CAN WE BE DECEIVED?

1. Does the Scripture teach the possibility of being deceived? *(Mark 13:5 "And Jesus answering them began to say, Take heed lest any man deceive you.")*

2. What does the devil do to the nations? *(Revelation 20:3 "And cast him into the bottomless pit, and shut him up, and set a seal upon him, that he should deceive the nations no more, till the thousand years should be fulfilled: and after that he must be loosed a little season.")*

3. List some things the Bible says about Cornelius? *(Acts 10:1, 2, 22 "There was a certain man in Caesarea called Cornelius, a centurion of the band called the Italian band, a devout man, and one that feared God with all his house, which gave much alms to the people, and prayed to God alway... And they said, Cornelius the centurion, a just man, and one that feareth God, and of good report among all the nation of the Jews, was warned from God by an holy angel to send for thee into his house, and to hear words of thee.")*

4. Does the Scripture indicate that he still lacked something? *(Acts 11:14 "Who shall tell thee words, whereby thou and all thy house shall be saved.")*

5. Who did God send to Cornelius? *(Acts 10:5 "And now send men to Joppa and call for one Simon, whose surname is Peter.")*

6. Although Cornelius was a fine religious man, was he saved before Peter came? *(Acts 11:12-14 "And the spirit bade me go with them, nothing doubting. Moreover these six brethren accompanied me, and we entered into the man's house: and he showed us how he had seen an angel in his house, which stood and said unto him, Send men to Joppa, and call for Simon, whose surname is Peter; who shall tell thee words, whereby thou and all thy house shall be saved.'")*

7. Is it possible to be religious and zealous of God yet not right with God? *(Romans 10:1-4 " Brethren, my heart's desire and prayer to God for Israel is, that they might be saved. For I bear them record that they have a zeal of God, but not according to knowledge. For they being ignorant of God's righteousness, and going about to establish their own righteousness, have not submitted themselves unto the righteousness of God. For Christ is the end of the law for righteousness to every one that believeth.")*

8. What was wrong with the zeal that these people had for God? *(Romans 10:2 above)*

9. Of what were these people unaware? *(Romans 10:3 "For they being ignorant of God's righteousness, and going*

*about to establish their own righteousness, have not submitted
themselves unto the righteousness of God."*

10. What did they substitute for God's
    righteousness? *(Romans 10:3 above)*

11. To what did they not submit or subject
    themselves unto? *(Romans 10: 3 above)*

12. What is the end of the law? *(Romans 10:4 "For
    Christ is the end of the law for righteousness to every one that
    believeth.")*

Part 6

IS SALVATION RELIGION OR CHRIST?

1. Did Philip tell the people of Samaria to join a
   particular church? *(Acts 8:5 "Then Philip went down to
   the city of Samaria, and preached Christ unto them.")*

2. What did Philip preach unto them? *(Acts 8:5
   above)*

3. What did the people do about Philip's
   preaching before they were baptized? *(Acts 8:12
   "But when they believed Philip preaching the things*

*concerning the kingdom of God, and the name of Jesus Christ,
they were baptized, both men and women."*)

4. What did the men of Cyprus and Cyrene preach to the people of Antioch? *(Acts 11:20 "And some of them were men of Cyprus and Cyrene, which, when they were come to Antioch, spake unto the Grecians, preaching the Lord Jesus."*)

5. What does Acts 11:21 emphasize that a great number of people did? *(Acts 11:21 "And the hand of the Lord was with them: and a great number believed, and turned unto the Lord."*)

6. When Barnabas came from Jerusalem, did he exhort these people to believe the teaching of any church? *(Acts 11:23 "Who, when he came, and had seen the grace of God, was glad, and exhorted them all, that with purpose of heart they would cleave unto the Lord."*)

7. Who did Barnabas exhort these people to cleave unto? *(Acts 11:23 "Who, when he came, and had seen the grace of God, was glad, and exhorted them all, that with purpose of heart they would cleave unto the Lord."*)

8. What church did Paul tell the Philippian jailer to join to be saved? *(Acts 16:28-31 "But Paul cried with a loud voice, saying, Do thyself no harm: for we are all here. Then he called for a light, and sprang in, and came trembling, and fell down before Paul and Silas, and brought them*

123

out, and said, Sirs, what must I do to be saved? And they said, Believe on the Lord Jesus Christ, and thou shalt be saved, and thy house.'")

9. What did Paul tell the Philippian jailer to do to be saved? *(Acts 16:28-31 above)*

10. What way did Jesus tell people to go to the Father? *(John 14:6 "Jesus saith unto him, I am the way, the truth, and the life: no man cometh unto the Father, but by me.")*

(Note: In Biblical Christianity people are always pointed to Christ for salvation and not to a church.)

Part 7

WHAT IS THE CRITERIA FOR HEAVEN?

1. What do you think a person has to do to go to heaven? Please give your own opinion.

2. Does a person go to heaven by good works? *(Ephesians 2:8, 9 "For by grace are ye saved through faith; and that not of yourselves: it is the gift of God: not of works, lest any man should boast.")*

3. Does a person go to heaven by obeying the law? (And by law the Scripture means the

124

commandments.) *(Galatians 2:16 "Knowing that a man is not justified by the works of the law, but by the faith of Jesus Christ, even we have believed in Jesus Christ, that we might be justified by the faith of Christ, and not by the works of the law: for by the works of the law shall no flesh be justified."*

4. What was the real purpose of the law? *(Romans 3:20 "Therefore by the deeds of the law there shall no flesh be justified in his sight: for by the law is the knowledge of sin.")*

5. What does the Law show us that we are before God? *(Romans 3:19 "Now we know that what things soever the law saith, it saith to them who are under the law: that every mouth may be stopped, and all the world may become guilty before God.")*

6. Is there anyone that is righteous enough in themselves to go to heaven? *(Romans 3:10, 23 "As it is written, There is none righteous, no, not one...." For all have sinned, and come short of the glory of God.")*

7. Does a person need to be baptized to go to heaven? *(Luke 23:39-43 "And one of the malefactors which were hanged railed on him, saying, If thou be Christ, save thyself and us. But the other answering rebuked him, saying, Dost not thou fear God, seeing thou art in the same condemnation? And we indeed justly; for we receive the due reward of our deeds: but this man hath done nothing amiss. And he said unto Jesus, Lord, remember me when thou comest into thy kingdom. And Jesus said unto him, Verily I say unto thee, Today shalt thou be with me in paradise.")*

8. Was Paul's mission from the Lord to go from town to town baptizing people? *(I Corinthians 1:17 "For Christ sent me not to baptize, but to preach the gospel: not with wisdom of words, lest the cross of Christ should be made of none effect.")*

9. God gives eternal life as a _____. *(Romans 6:23 "For the wages of sin is death; but the gift of God is eternal life through Jesus Christ our Lord.")*

10. How does the Bible say we get eternal life or the assurance of heaven? *(Acts 16:31 "And they said, Believe on the Lord Jesus Christ, and thou shalt be saved...")* (Also see Ephesians 2:8, 9 above in question 2.)

11. Can we buy the gift? *(Acts 8:20 "But Peter said unto him, Thy money perish with thee, because thou hast thought that the gift of God may be purchased with money.")*

12. Can we know while we are on earth that we have eternal life? *(I John 5:13 "These things have I written unto you that believe on the name of the Son of God; that ye may know that ye have eternal life, and that ye may believe on the name of the Son of God.")*

13. What has God given to us? *(I John 5:11 "And this is the record, that God hath given to us eternal life, and this life is in his Son.")*

14. Where is this life? *(I John 5:11 above)*

15. Who has this life? *(I John 5:12 "He that hath the Son hath life; and he that hath not the Son of God hath not life.")*

16. Who does not have this life? *(I John 5:12 above)*

17. Would you like to know how you can have eternal life?

Part 8

BIBLICAL SALVATION

1. What are Jews and Gentiles all under? *(Romans 3:9 "What then? Are we better than they? No, in no wise: for we have before proved both Jews and Gentiles, that they are all under sin.")* (The word "Gentiles means non-jews.)

2. What does God say are the negative characteristics of the human race? *(Romans 3:10-12 "As it is written, There is none righteous, no, not one: There is none that understandeth, there is none that seeketh after God. They are all gone out of the way, they are together become unprofitable; there is none that doeth good, no, not one.")*

3. How does Romans 3:23 apply to you? *(Romans 3:23 "For all have sinned, and come short of the glory of God.")*

4. What are the wages we will receive because

of our sin? *(Romans 6:23 "For the wages of sin is death; but the gift of God is eternal life through Jesus Christ our Lord.")*

5. **Who has already paid those wages?** *(Romans 5:8 "But God commendeth his love toward us, in that, while we were yet sinners, Christ died for us.") (I Corinthians15:3 "For I delivered unto you first of all that which I also received, how that Christ died for our sins according to the scriptures.") (I Peter 2:24 "Who his own self bare our sins in his own body on the tree, that we, being dead to sins, should live unto righteousness: by whose stripes ye were healed.")*

6. **Although Christ has already been punished for your sins, what does God ask of you?** *(Acts 20:21 "Testifying both to the Jews, and also to the Greeks, repentance toward God, and faith toward our Lord Jesus Christ.")*

7. **How can you exercise faith in Christ?** *(John 1:12 "But as many as received him, to them gave he power to become the sons of God, even to them that believe on his name.") (I John 5:12 "He that hath the Son hath life; and he that hath not the Son of God hath not life.")*

Would you like to receive Christ as your Savior? If you would, then:
(1) Acknowledge that you are a sinner and in need of Christ.
(2) Thank Christ for dying on the cross for your sin.
(3) Ask Christ to come into you heart and be your Savior and Lord.
